T0158890

MATRIXWORKS

A Life-Affirming Guide to Facilitation Mastery and Group Genius

Mukara Meredith,
with Lisa Rome

BALBOA.
PRESS

A DIVISION OF HAY HOUSE

Balboa Press books may be ordered through booksellers or by contacting:

Balboa Press
A Division of Hay House
1663 Liberty Drive
Bloomington, IN 47403
www.balboapress.com
1 (877) 407-4847

Because of the dynamic nature of the Internet, any web addresses or links contained in this book may have changed since publication and may no longer be valid. The views expressed in this work are solely those of the author and do not necessarily reflect the views of the publisher, and the publisher hereby disclaims any responsibility for them.

The author of this book does not dispense medical advice or prescribe the use of any technique as a form of treatment for physical, emotional, or medical problems without the advice of a physician, either directly or indirectly. The intent of the author is only to offer information of a general nature to help you in your quest for emotional and spiritual well-being. In the event you use any of the information in this book for yourself, which is your constitutional right, the author and the publisher assume no responsibility for your actions.

Any people depicted in stock imagery provided by Thinkstock are models, and such images are being used for illustrative purposes only.
Certain stock imagery © Thinkstock.

Print information available on the last page.

ISBN: 978-1-5043-7467-5 (sc)
ISBN: 978-1-5043-7469-9 (hc)
ISBN: 978-1-5043-7468-2 (e)

Library of Congress Control Number: 2017902192

Balboa Press rev. date: 07/15/2017

Contents

Dedication

Dedication of Merit

Our intention is to relieve unnecessary suffering in individuals, groups, teams, and organizations. We dedicate the merit of this work to the cultivation of well-being. May all that live continue to thrive.

Acknowledgements

Many teachers, traditions, experiences and insights have influenced this continuously evolving work. My intention is to credit and express appreciation for all who have taught me and the entire MatrixWorks Faculty: especially those teachers who have given a deeper connection to Ancient Wisdom Traditions and those students who have made the teachings come alive through our interpersonal connections.

Mukara wishes to acknowledge Amina Knowlin and David Patterson for their creation of the Group Leadership Training in the late nineties, as this was the beginning of the creation of MatrixWorks. More recently, the work of Thomas Huebl has deepened the MatrixWorks understanding of the role of subtle energy in powerful group work.

Mukara offers a deep bow of gratitude for the Hakomi system and the MatrixHakomi Team for helping me learn more fully the lessons of how to belong and to be autonomous simultaneously in healthy ways.

In truth, this book owes its existence to the skill, love and commitment of many: Most especially Lisa Rome, for her commitment to bringing MatrixWorks into the world and birthing this book. Sarah Lila Oswald, for her everlasting support in bringing MatrixWorks into the 21st century, and personal support to Mukara as I travel around the world. Anne Parker, for her vision and dedication to recognizing and championing the value of relationship as integral to environmental work. Anna Chitty, for our co-teaching and collaboration in the early days of MatrixWorks. Rebecca Smith-Woody, for helping me recognize the systems aspect of MatrixWorks as the medicine needed for these times. Jaci Hull, for supporting the integration of Hakomi and

MatrixWorks, and our wild teaching adventures in Brazil. Lael Keen and Russell Jones, for bringing MatrixWorks to Brazil in 2004 and for integrating MatrixWorks principles and practices into their somatic teachings throughout the world. Ivy Ross, leader, designer, and human being extraordinaire, for believing in MatrixWorks (and me) in 1999, and launching my career in the conscious business world. And especially for my partner in life and evolution: Shano Kelley.

I am grateful for the spiritual guidance, living example, and inspiration that I've received from Sangye Khandro and Lama Yeshe Wangmo. And to all beings that have added strengths and provided challenges across my path along the way, I am grateful.

May all beings be well and happy. May we all benefit from a deeper understanding of how human systems can become living systems, so that we may live in a more life-affirming world.

Introduction

G rowth is an impulse of all living beings. It is the primary movement and expression of anything alive. In people and groups, we see this represented as the evolutionary impulse: a pattern of coherence that guides the universe and all beings towards enlightenment. Wherever there's a spark, whether creative or destructive, that is the evolutionary impulse trying to set the conditions for the next level of growth and healing trying to happen. Living systems follow this impulse by nature, and we believe that human beings can re-learn how to access this potential through intentional group work.

MatrixWorks[1] is a revolutionary process that utilizes principles of New Science, Whole Systems Thinking, Hakomi Psychotherapy,[2] Spirituality, and Contemporary Psychology to understand and support the growth and development of healthy functioning groups and individuals. At its core, MatrixWorks exists to teach groups how to thrive as living systems, and individuals to take leadership in their groups and lives. This book gives you the teaching frameworks to create this aliveness in yourself and the groups in which you participate.

As conscientious beings (and we include you, our lovely reader!) we have seen groups, teams, and organizations fail to access this evolutionary potential. We wrote this book because we know more is possible with the right kind of skillful intervention. We believe that human beings are basically good, but the structures and organizations we create do not always reflect this essential basic goodness. Power dynamics, carelessness, and abuses of resources contribute to issues like the economic crisis, the climate crisis, poverty, war, gender, race, and sexuality. We believe they can be solved by intentional human compassion. At this point in the world's evolution, we have no choice. More than ever, the quality of our lives depends on our ability to work together and care for planet.

MatrixWorks is a new model of leadership that teaches the collective cultivation of values, skills and capacities that are uniquely human as the primary tools for leaders.

To accomplish this end, MatrixWorks utilizes the following teaching frameworks, organized as sections throughout the book:

- Living Systems Theory applied to groups.
- How to serve life through the spirals of connection and inclusion, conflict and chaos, and creative evolution and consciousness.
- How to develop the capacities for self-organization, self-referencing, self-correcting, and self-generating.
- Integration of scientific and subjective perspectives. Using mindfulness practice, emotional intelligence, and neuroscience to enrich (instead of contradict) each other.
- Four pillars of the inner world: Paying attention to how feelings bridge the inner, relational, and field perceptions.
- Five principles of creating healthy relationships.
- Ground, Path, and Fruit: This book is organized into three parts following this Buddhist framework for understanding reality. The ground corresponds to our theoretical framework, the path corresponds to our facilitation training and group practices, and the fruit relates to the practical application of MatrixWorks in the world.

These models are of a fractal nature. Fractals are complex patters that are self-similar across micro and macro scales. This natural phenomenon is exemplified by the structure of a tree, which mimics the micro scale of a leaf in the macro scale of the roots and branches. Fractal nature means that if something is true, then it is true at all levels of scale (cellular, individual, group, organization, and planet). When we use these models to facilitate healing in our lives and groups, we can see the effects ripple out in fractal patterns.

From these frameworks, we hold a developmental map of how evolution happens. The most essential need of all living beings, and therefore our most essential task in creating groups that work, is health and growth. We are here to witness the great perfection of life itself, and the recognition of our own awake-ness. Everything living already has a basic Buddha nature, which is access to consciousness that leads to enlightenment. MatrixWorks exists to offer a glimpse at the steps along the way to the great perfection. We've used this method to develop healing and growth for individuals, relationships, communities, and workplaces. Time and experience shows us that we have a model of group dynamics facilitation that works. We're going to help you see *how* it works and *why* it works, so you can practice it in your life and leadership.

If growth is the primary impulse of living beings, we can start to look outside the box towards what kind of growth is healthy, and what kind of growth supports and nurtures life. As a global society, we have learned how to support the growth of things we create: companies, profits, wealth, products, and agriculture. Yet we are still learning how to grow our relationships and a healthy sense of self. We are still learning how to support the health of our planet. MatrixWorks can help facilitators weave matrices as wombs that grow the new individual to better relate and create.

MatrixWorks is a lived experience in constant evolution. It cannot be digested all at once, nor without practice and practical application. Take it slow. You may not get it all at once. Visit us at MatrixWorks.org to join the conversation, find classes, request a facilitator, or ask us specific questions about how to guide your group relationships towards health.

Transformation cannot be consumed. It can only be embodied. MatrixWorks follows a tempo: learning, becoming aware, and practicing transformative healing. To get the most out of this book, we recommend reading through the whole book to gather a gestalt of the concepts, then going back to the practices as needed. Our teachings will be more useful by integrating the practices.

The practices take on an evolutionary nature once you've integrated the learning. As you master the learning material, you'll find that you're able to create and invent practices of your own that directly apply to the context of your own groups.

Through these practices, we learn how to be led by something larger. We learn the path of the Bodhisattva, one who acts for the benefit of the whole. Many of us haven't experienced essential basic goodness, and that's why we feel suffering and get stuck in our group relationships. We're here to re-awaken safety that leads to enlightenment for groups. We're not here to tell you the answers, but rather to show you that the wisdom is already within you.

Before we embark into the theory, our first task is to develop safety. So first, let's take a moment for self-reflection and mindfulness. You'll find these practices at the end of every chapter, designed to help you integrate the material from that section.

Practice: Connect, first, with yourself...

Feel into your heart and your response to yourself just now. In this moment, you might be feeling a sense of ease, or perhaps you are a little nervous. Maybe there is excitement and a quality of joy. Or, perhaps a quality of calmness and peace. Whatever you feel or sense is okay. We are just taking time to be mindful--for you to notice your interior life. So, take a few moments more to connect with yourself.

To complete this first part, if it feels right to you, place your right hand on your heart. If your hand could speak, what would it say to your heart? If your heart could speak, what might it say to your hand? Allow the answers to emerge gently from your deep mind. Receive them as the gift they are.

Now that you are resourced with yourself, we will share more of our approach to MatrixWorks Leadership.

Reflection Questions:

What attracted you to this book? What drew you to explore groups as living systems? What are your learning intentions? What are your current assumptions about MatrixWorks?

Mukara's Story

I came to this work at an early age. I grew up in the Deep South, an only child raised by my grandparents, who were Baptist preachers. There was a lot of flux and change in my home environment; I was exposed to several different family settings because of my mother's mental illness. Moving around I had many different family experiences with many different norms; I never felt like I understood how to belong or had a home of belonging. At the time, there were no support groups or systems to strengthen her health. This lack of belonging and the sense of not knowing that I had a place created in me a sense of isolation and separation. It was my deep need to be part of a matrix (meaning: womb or mother) that motivated what became my life's work.

I spent a lot of my time with my grandparents in church, visiting the sick, and experiencing a generational gap that left me longing for deep connection. I wanted to fit in, to belong in a group. I kept making relationship messes, so I had to learn how to relate better before I got myself hurt. The old adage "we teach what we need to learn" applies here. My loneliness was so great that I had to find a way to make family. Looking back on my unmet need for a matrix of connection, I recognize that I tried to meet my needs by turning to spirituality. As I worked on healing myself through Buddhist learning and practice, I realized that I still needed to bring this healing into my life and relationships. It was easy to feel nourished through my individual meditation practices, but I couldn't hide from my pain nor change the realities of my personal life. Part of my learning became using my spirituality as a resource, but not ignoring my pain of isolation. Through the practice of healing my relationships, and myself, I learned to create the conditions that might have helped my mother's own healing.

As I started my professional life in social work, I began to witness similar pains in others. Wounds are quickly created in groups when we don't understand differences in personalities, roles, and power. As a social worker, I learned how to create for my clients the conditions of healing that I was learning for myself. From my childhood experience with the pain of aloneness, I saw how powerful the role of connection could be for others, and that became the guiding principle for my professional journey.

The first 'group' I ever did was in 1968 with several African American women in Lafayette, Louisiana. They were each in a training to get off welfare by becoming nurses assistants in hospitals. Working with these women individually, I realized that their problems and pains were all the same as anyone else: wanting to be seen, to be heard, and to be a part of something larger. They didn't have a matrix of connection among themselves. There had never been a group done in Lafayette, and I decided to do a group with them. I didn't even know what a group was but I knew we needed to do it. This was prior to my Master's Degree in social work, so I was truly a novice about group work at the time. I just understood intuitively that if I got them together, they would support each other (and personally, that it would serve the same need I knew I needed). It was amazing to see these women transform through the cultivation of healthy relationships, translate these skills into thriving work relationships, and step into their power at work. I knew we were on to something when I watched them on their last day of our training *choose* to walk through the entrance that all of the hospital workers walked through, instead of through the back entrance that they were accustomed to. Experiencing the small transformation that this group manifested was an emotional experience for me. I felt a sense of their triumph. I experienced gratitude to have personal contact with the transformative process. Some deep part of my being felt I was more connected to my purpose in life.

My personal connection to this group was the beginning seed for MatrixWorks, and it led to my work evolution. This experience prompted me to attend graduate school in social work, where I earned a scholarship because of my work with adolescent welfare clients. I continued to be fascinated by groups. Part of my graduate work involved implementing groups at the maternal clinic where I practiced. For eight years, I provided emotional support to low-income pregnant women (specifically adolescents) who needed the support of connection in a clinical setting as they navigated their pregnancies alone. These experiences led to the creation of MatrixWorks, a simple model for how groups can become a living system where the whole is greater than the sum of the parts. What's radical about this is not so much the theory, but the direct feeling of being safe, being welcomed, and being fully yourself in a group. This is a life-changing experience that every human being deserves.

From 1999 to 2012 I devoted a lot of time and MatrixWorks energy to the business world. I had read an article that said business could save the world, and I got on the bus. I worked with corporate teams around the world, and saw much success. I eventually transitioned when the leader of one large corporate client told me he liked the work I was doing, but it would never catch on because he couldn't lead in this way. I became disillusioned. He was knowingly willing to limit the benefits for his employees because of his own limitations and unwillingness to learn. I took some time off to have a knee surgery, so I wasn't traveling, and I started to question the value of working in business. I made the decision to work only with companies where consciousness is a part of their mandate. It closed some doors for MatrixWorks, but it also opened up new possibilities in gathering together groups of people who sought this relational leadership. In my own evolution as a catalyst for change, I found myself drawn to the role of women in the transformation needed in society. I made the commitment to teach Enlightened Feminine Leadership courses to bring legitimacy to these skills and capacities associated with women. I put my anchor in the ground for consciousness, and I still hold for that. I now only work with leaders who recognize consciousness and balance as necessary conditions for society to change.

As a 108-year-old Tibetan elf (that's my personal archetype), I choose to allocate my energy in this direction. It's my calling to integrate the one and the many. I remember a time about 10 years ago when my meditation teacher wanted me to begin to guide people in the traditional Tibetan Buddhist path, and I said to her "I can't do that. I was given this job to make a system that is easy for people to relate and I want to be true to that. It's not that meditation isn't important, but just to sit on the cushion means that I'm limited in teaching my calling of 'integrating the temple with the marketplace' (inspired by Thomas

Hubel)." I still believe that it is time to bring these two together, to reintegrate the parts back to the whole of life. We are reaching for what feels more true and necessary in terms of our evolution. I feel hard times are going to come and the only way to make it through is if we can be together and if we can see ourselves in other people. Knowing about group dynamics changes how you are in every group. The ability to take on the perspective of the other is a crucial skill in working well together.

What I've discovered through my journey is the truth of the statement "the gift is in every wound." Looking back on my life I understand some of the early experiences of loneliness and disconnection truly propelled me to try to find a way to support individual and collective evolution and transformation. According to Mother Theresa, "All of our problems stem from the fact that we have forgotten that we belong together." My journey has been a remembering and embodying the truth that we belong together and this togetherness can be life affirming.

Lisa's Story

Well-being, communication, nature, and wholeness are the threads woven throughout my life and work endeavors. Growing up in the Midwest, I had an appreciation for the rooting values of family, hard work, and integrity, but often felt there was a part of my spirit yearning to be expressed. Without an evolved social structure, I struggled to flourish in a fully embodied way. This catalyzed my quest to seek out different models of learning and leadership, ultimately guiding me to MatrixWorks and Mukara. Studying and facilitating with Mukara over these years has been a divine treat, one that led to many afternoons asking interview questions over Bengal Spice tea that would ultimately lead to the creation of this book.

Through my evolution as a ski instructor, health and wellness writer, environmental leader, and workplace culture change consultant, I've become aware of the ways relationships – healthful relationships with self, other, and nature – can shape our ability to thrive, do better, accomplish more, and live a meaningful life. MatrixWorks has given me the tools to bring this power into the workforce so that work can be a force for good.

In the search for a kinder world, we can all stand to be a little kinder to ourselves and each other. Conflict, differences, and stuck-ness will arise even in groups of well-meaning and best-intentioned individuals. Creative magic happens when we find ways to be fully ourselves and a member of a diverse community. I'm honored to make these principles and practices of group matrix-weaving available to serve the evolution of the world, through your hands.

This book is a reflection of the teachings, facilitation, and ethos of MatrixWorks, told in first person perspectives from Mukara. It is a living manual: constantly evolving and intended to be digested in the way that serves you best. I'm grateful to have been able to provide the organizing structure and form to Mukara's gifts of teaching. It is shared as a loving offering to the work of healing ourselves, each other, and the whole universe. I hope you receive the benefits of deep connection as I have.

Part One
The Ground: Theory

Basic Goodness

When everything else is taken away, what is left of the human being, what's true of the human being are the qualities of Loving Kindness, Joy, Compassion, and Equanimity. These can never be taken away.
- Tharthang Tulku, Rinpoche Nyingma Institute

MatrixWorks operates from the principle that humans are born to love. Yet due to circumstances beyond our control, we sometimes need to relearn embodying love in our lives. Groups are like living, breathing organisms that have the potential to nourish and innovate. Yet in our industrial society, groups sometimes get confused for the machines that dominate our daily experience, and people get confused for replaceable parts. This confusion can sap the life force from a group and its members. The core of MatrixWorks is to help groups reach their potential as fully functioning, thriving, living systems: systems where no one is replaceable, and everyone has an integral part to play in the evolution of the whole. As living systems, all parts are essential and cannot be replaced, relationships are the currency of energy, and the task is called forth as creative evolutionary purpose (not solely profit, although that's important too). This organic nature of a group is basic goodness.

Before any offering of MatrixWorks opens up, a ground of loving presence begins to open. I begin to tune in to a portal of possibilities for the group. This ground is the essential element of any transformative experience, as the seed of an organism carries within the outline of the whole unfolding. There are many components of this ground, the most essential being the beliefs and intention of those creating it. The Bill O'Brien quote "the success of an intervention depends upon the interior condition of the intervener" deeply resonates with how I approach working with a group. It is what I learned working with the women in Lafayette early in my career. In the initial ground of possibilities for a group, I touch a place where I know human beings are good and they can be good together. The energy I'm opening is commitment to the experience of being good and being even better together. This is well described by a memory I have of attending a talk by Stephen Porges, a leader in bridging the study of neuroscience with social behavior theory. Before he began the lecture, he took a moment to make eye contact with every person in the audience. Then he said the words that I always remember and that continue to guide me. "Human beings are good, and good human beings deserve to know what's going on inside them." I fell totally in love when he said that. That moment of authentic connection created a ground of safety that is essential to the MatrixWorks experience.

A veil hangs over basic goodness like a cloud that blocks the light of the sun. This veil contributes to the perception of separation between group members and the benefit of the whole. Like the ego, it sends the message that all needs cannot be met, and that needs must be met at the expense of another. Many group experiences foster this sense of toxic separation, rather than the inherent health of basic goodness. Since separation leads to suffering, group dynamics can be painful. MatrixWorks explores the nature of suffering and how to end unnecessary suffering through the practical application of Buddhism.

The word *Buddha* means to wake up. In all Buddhist traditions, there is the idea that we can rest into, and take refuge in, the Buddha. In addition to the capacity to wake up, this includes the dharma, (commitment to truth), and the Sangha (the community of people who want to wake up and commit to truth together). Many teachers have said that in the West we don't know how to cultivate the jewel of the Sangha, and this MatrixWorks offering is a map to do so. If the next

Buddha is the Sangha, as Zen master Thich Nhat Hanh says, then we are here to awaken through small groups by building connection and creating a world that works. The fundamental ground of MatrixWorks is the understanding of interconnectedness through the direct experience of belonging together.

I became involved in business in the 1990's, when a former client finished therapy with me after working together for eighteen months, and said, "We need what you do in business. We need help making the workplace more human." At the time, my work in business was a radical concept, whereas now many companies have their own programs for mindfulness and group dynamics. So when I started bringing Hakomi and MatrixWorks into business, I came in through the design and innovation departments that were already looking for what's outside the box and open to "disruptive innovation." My unique selling position was the insight that if they wanted to innovate, they had to learn to be together at work in a different way. I led these groups through the three spirals of connection, chaos, and creative expression (described in a following chapter). My goal was to unleash the genius of each team and foster an experience of how the intelligence and creativity were distributed throughout all members of the team. By including more than yourself into your consciousness, you transcend differences and relax in basic goodness. When no one of us is as smart as all of us, we experience the merits of basic goodness.

Basic goodness guides us to begin every encounter by assuming innocence and purity at the core of every being. Yes, we accumulate wounds and egos over a lifetime, but basic goodness reminds us that there is always perfection underneath. My teacher Chogyam Trungpa Rinpoche taught that basic goodness is a condition of being alive.

To facilitate life-affirming group genius in a MatrixWorks way, hold the compass of basic goodness to guide your efforts and intuition back home to this essential perfection. You can use this concept to remind people of the love that is possible when we see each other and are seen as we truly are.

We often use meditation and body awareness to first bring people into this connection of their own basic goodness. When people settle into their own basic goodness, we then guide them towards seeing goodness in others.

Basic goodness is sufficient in itself to guide a group of individuals back to health and creative evolution, and the following chapters provide further tools for healing the wounds and cutting the veils that hinder our experience of this basic perfection.

Reflection Questions

What is your experience of basic goodness? What is your commitment to "waking up"? How do these principles relate to your own beliefs and traditions?

Living Systems

A human being is a part of the whole, called by us the 'Universe,' a part limited in time and space. He experiences himself; his thoughts and feelings as something separate from the rest--a kind of optical illusion of his consciousness. This delusion is a kind of prison for us, restricting us to our personal desires and to affection for a few persons nearest to us. Our task must be to free ourselves from the prison by widening our circle of compassion to embrace all living creatures and the whole of nature in its beauty...The striving for such achievement is in itself a part of the liberation and a foundation for inner security.
- Albert Einstein

Aristotle first used the phrase "The whole is greater than the sum of its parts," which is the main definition of a living system. Living systems are organisms defined by three properties: communion, diversity, and self-creation. A system is a collection of parts that interact with each other to function as a whole. This informs our work with groups because we are straying from the traditional industrial model of seeing groups as machines and transitioning toward seeing groups as alive and full of potential to serve the whole of life.

Living systems thrive under these conditions. In my work with Hakomi, a body-based psychotherapy practice, I learned to treat the body as a living system. Hakomi means: "How do you stand in relation to all that is?" It is a method for understanding who you are in the universe, and developing loving acceptance of the part you play in your relationship to the whole. We can access the basic goodness of living systems by using body-awareness. Our bodies are the most immediate and intimate living system we have contact with. Within our bodies are parts within parts, systems within systems that are whole in themselves and also make up larger wholes. What this means for us is that we can look to the body as both a metaphor and reality for how living systems distribute intelligence throughout all parts of their system.

MatrixWorks has been described as the art and science of learning to work with groups as living systems. With MatrixWorks, I apply this framework to groups and group dynamics. Hakomi treats the human body and self as a living system, and MatrixWorks treats the group as a body that is also living system. This work has evolved through the study and practical application of chaos and complexity theory, Hakomi, Buddhism, somatic psychology, the group leadership training, and the universal healing principles of biodynamic cranial work. The laboratory of experience for this model has been group process classes at Naropa University, the highly creative design teams at Mattel Toy division, and ongoing MatrixWorks trainings at my office in Boulder and around the globe.

The following is a chart comparing the Seven Organic Principles of Living Systems, by Mark Youngblood (shown in the left column), to the MatrixWorks underlying assumptions that form the "ground" of working groups as living systems (shown in the right column). Viewing a group from this ground will positively affect the life of the group. As you read them, consider how you feel as you imagine working in a group that would reflect these principles. Consider what groups in your life already follow these principles and what principles could benefit your existing groups.

Living Systems:	Groups:
Wholeness Systems are "wholes" with properties that are emergent (i.e., greater than the sum of their parts). Systems cannot be reduced to the operation and characteristics of the individual components.	**Basic Goodness** At the core of every individual and group is a basic goodness. Goodness manifests as qualities of compassion, love, generosity, and joy.
Connectedness Systems are indivisibly interconnected in complex, non-linear ways. The intricate connectedness of living systems makes it virtually impossible to establish and understand clear causes and effects.	**Everything is Interconnected** Nothing happens in isolation. Things arise in relationship to each other. "Nothing is itself without everything else." Networks of connection are the underlying pattern of all living systems.
Identity A system organizes around a central idea, a strong identity and sense of purpose that transcends its changing structure. Agents in a system have substantial autonomy and act in self-assertive ways, but their actions are integrative and in harmony with the whole. The agents are guided in their actions to maintain the whole by a few organizing principles.	**Fundamental Health** We are all expressions of health. An individual and a group are always expressing as much health as possible in any given moment; if the health is observed, it will express more clearly.

Balance	**Intelligence**
Living systems establish a dynamic balance – a fluctuating stability that is far from equilibrium – among its key parameters. Living systems seek to optimize, not to maximize.	Living Systems have the intelligence, wisdom and resources within them that they need to self-organize, learn, and grow.
Creativity	**Evolutionary Intelligence**
Although most small changes and disturbances are suppressed through negative feedback, certain novel and creative changes are amplified by the system as positive feedback. Feedback systems, then, both maintain the system through self-renewal, and cause it to evolve to whole new levels of order and complexity through self- transcendence. This ability to form whole new levels of order is Nature's true source of creativity.	We have an underlying sanity that is brilliant. We exist in a field that is coherent in nature. There is a treatment plan inherent within an individual and a group that will unfold towards health if we listen to and support it. Individuals and groups are organized by an intelligence that is evolutionary in nature. Living Systems access their deep and creative intelligence by cultivating and developing their networks of connection directly in group contexts.

Openness Creativity in systems is increased through three factors: (1) the agents in the system interact extensively both internally and externally, (2) information is rich and diverse and flows freely, and (3) there is tremendous diversity in the system, which is expressed through the agents. Stability is maintained through identity, boundaries, canalization, and maladaptive learning.	**Living Systems** All Human systems are Living Systems. This applies to bodies, individuals, families, groups, and organizations.
Flexibility There is tremendous plasticity and flexibility in the system. Processes and flows constantly organize structures to match environmental conditions.	**Healing Happens in the Present** When this intelligence is accessed, real transformation is possible: for the individual, group, family, organization, and society. Transformation means a fundamental change in the quality of relationships within the system.

The organic principles in the left column begin to inform our understanding of how living systems work. The MatrixWorks principles in the right column provide a collective agreement for how a group can understand its own health or lack thereof. Using these principles in the right column to assess the life of a group is an informal way to begin to see the system of the group.

Living systems provide the framework for understanding how a group can come back to life after falling flat. It can be used as a diagnostic tool for understanding what needs to change. When we come into partnership with the organic nature of living systems, our organizations naturally shift to support the life of those within and to nurture the life outside the organization. Teaching the framework of living systems reminds group members that we are all living, that life is precious, and that our groups and organizations as a whole can become more life affirming. In MatrixWorks, we set up structures and practices to honor the uniqueness of every group member, while nurturing the connections between each person, and nudging the group along a creative endeavor. Simply making this evident as group guidelines and agreements can go a long way. Paying attention to health as a group guides the group towards life, just as paying attention to the breath through meditation deepens breathing.

Joanna Macy and Michelle Holiday have worked to bridge living systems awareness with environmental activism. They offer a simple definition of living systems that illuminates our paradigm: all living systems are made up of different parts, all those parts come together to make a convergent whole, those parts exist in dynamic relationships, in a fundamental pattern where they are continually creating, changing, and evolving themselves, in order to serve life. The last part is why I love their work so much. Without serving life as the aspiration and imperative, living systems don't find their fulfillment. I see this evidenced in the groups that do find fulfillment: the ability to make everything better in groups as living systems comes from serving something larger than ourselves. This is true for everything from the human body, to groups, to nature, to anything living. The challenge for those of us who care about healing in our time is figuring out how to make serving life an essential component for engaging with the world.

Living systems carry an innate intelligence that is greater than anything we could invent without them. Living systems create from within. This contrasts with the mechanistic understanding where things have to be fixed by an external source. A machine can't create living systems. They have their own DNA and organizing principle. In a living system, the wisdom exists within the group and the system is able to repair itself. The locust of power is within the living system, whereas in the mechanical system the source of life is generated from someone operating it. We're at a place where the world will be served if we look at everything as if it were living, and stop de-humanizing so many aspects of our lives. For example, if I cut my finger, the body knows exactly what to do. The doctor is a facilitator of healing, but not the healer itself. If my car breaks, it is not going to heal itself. We have all the technology to heal already!

The most important take away is that living systems serve life. All living systems have the capacity to learn, grow, and evolve. As a facilitator, my prime motivation is igniting the livingness of any group. This approach with living systems allows us to continually reach out to our future selves. Living systems remind us of the hidden potential to update who we are, and our commitment to serving life.

If there is a team that gels and comes together as a living system, then something about the relational field takes on a quality of deep connection and begins to highlight the power of any relationship to be a healing relationship.

> **Practice:** Pause and reflect on groups you're a part of and active with now. Where are these principles present and not present? Where are there parts that have converged to make a new whole? Of all the groups, how are they serving life? How is life being fulfilled? How might this deeper understanding of the group as a living system influence your capacity to facilitate in a more living way, as a place where healing happens? Can we always open to the healing impulse and allow something new to emerge?

Reflection Questions: What is a living system, and why is it important? Why is it a leadership model for these times? Start with the components of living systems that are important to understand in your organization and leadership.

5 friends
An Essential Equation for Group Health

As the saying goes, we get by with a little help from our friends. Likewise, we don't get very far without our friends. We've identified five 'friends' that are necessary for group genius to emerge. Each of the friends has a corresponding competency to practice along with it. Without true friends, it's challenging to enjoy life and our relationships lack nourishment. With these friends, we can open up to unleashing the creative genius within each member and the group as a whole.

Group life follows the same pattern as the developmental growth cycle in a human. Starting in infancy, it moves to childhood, adolescence, adulthood, elderhood and eventually death. Like an infant, group life reaches developmental cycles in sequence. Each of the five friends and corresponding five competencies builds upon the previous one in this developmental sequence. Any trauma or drama will pause the growth process, leaving the individual or group in a cycle of suspended healing. In MatrixWorks, we put intention into the initial conditions of group life by attending to developmental needs, just as you would for a child. The attention to detail and care signals to the group unconscious that it is safe to grow.

The five friends engender vulnerability, precision, and ease. We introduce these friends as an exercise in asking for what you need, and becoming what's needed in an evolutionary relationship. Use the five friends to identify what your needs are, how people can help meet your needs, and how you can help meet the needs of others. We're able to accomplish much more when we feel cared for.

5 Friends

To optimize positive patterns in your Relationships, learn to use these magical keys. These 5 friends represent feeling qualities that, if present, allow people in groups to let go of a sense of separateness. A healthy, inclusive, and evolutionary group will contain these qualities.

- **Safety:** developing Safety in self, group, culture, and planet. Absolute safety doesn't exist. Relative safety means that the conditions needed for not having to worry about safety are met. These conditions are the conditions of the Social Nervous System: Listening and looking (face-to-face) connection. There is little safety without a felt-sense of connection to self, other and the Larger. If safety is okay and connections are flowing we are less afraid of conflict.
- **Support:** the elegance of providing support. True support is in contrast to false strength or helplessness. The key is connecting themes from the group (e.g. being seen, being named). "I can go and give support if I feel I'm going to be received"
- **Creative Expression and Freedom:** becoming the creator of your own destiny. Self-Expression vs. being controlled by others and feeling stuck. Creativity to be different.
- **Truth:** cutting through veils of ignorance to reveal a larger Truth with a capital "T". Genuine uniqueness vs. false persona to fit the context we're trying to manipulate.
- **Value and Worth:** value and worth at the core of everything allows spaciousness to emerge. Grounded in being vs. proving our worth by what we can accomplish.

Each of the friends above has its own guiding competency to work with. The 5 competencies show us how to take incoherent energy and move it to enlightenment. These represent a developmental map for the evolutionary process that applies to human development, group development, and movement of energy toward enlightenment (An enhanced capacity for self-awareness and for collective awareness). Cultivating these competencies will result in leadership actions that meet the genuine needs of the situations we are faced with. Drawn from a Buddhist map called the Four Karmas, these competencies provide us with a basic tool kit of skillful means that function like banks of the river, supporting the river to flow in ways that serve the individuals and the whole systems. The 5 friends are WHAT you are cultivating in the individuals and the group; the 5 competencies are HOW you can cultivate these as the group develops.

Competency One: Peace Making *(other words to describe are: Ground, Stabilize, Meet).*

This competency directs us to assume an attitude of Grounding and Stabilizing. We welcome all the emotional energy and information that is part of the situation we face. Listening deeply and without reaction, we become receptive to what is trying to emerge. We establish a field of safety and non-judgment, transforming chaos into workability.

This competency allows us to join with whatever is happening so that we bring a quality of 'peace-making' and calmness to the situation. This is not about placating or accommodating, but more like being willing to welcome all the information and emotional energy that is part of the complex. An attitude on non-resistance and openness is expressed in this competency. The ability to listen deeply and be non-reactive on the part of the Leader supports the power of this first competency. At this stage, we get clearer about what the issue is, become more receptive to what action may be needed, and what is trying to emerge. We establish Safety and a field of non-blame, which brings resource and sanity to the system.

Competency Two: Enriching *(other words to describe are: Invite, Hidden Potential, Beauty, Goodness, Many Voices)*

This Competency encourages us to orient to situations with an attitude of 'Uplifting' the energy we encounter. We may ask: "What gift of art, beauty, or generosity might enhance or increase the energetic potency of any situation?" Sometimes, we may enrich leadership challenges by inviting all voices to be heard.

This second competency allows us to focus on what is present and what is absent in the situation. We become curious about how might we 'enrich' or 'increase' the situation we are dealing with. We can think of this capacity as a kind of 'gift giving' as we are intent here on uplifting the energy and increasing the feeling of ease and relaxation. Two of the most important 'gifts' at this phase are: a) *Space* and b) *Contact.* Discerning which of these is needed is crucial to being able to use this capacity in the most powerful way. If contact is needed, we engage completely. If Space is needed, we may initiate a pause and literally give the situation some space. In a more tangible way, sometimes changing the environment with the addition of Art: adding flowers or introducing nourishing food can stimulate the experience of enrichment as a leadership competency. Inviting all voices to join the conversation is another tangible way to practice enrichment as a leadership competency.

Competency Three: Magnetizing *(other words to describe are: Calling Forth New Possibilities, Flirting with the Unknown, Spontaneous Arising, Emergence)*

This competency helps us establish nourishing relationships. Our genuine warm-heartedness helps us build teams, organizations and tribes that care for each other and the whole. Through magnetizing energy, we open to the magic of new possibilities and surprising emergences. Our loving is powerful and our power is loving.

This competency allows us to include an openness to magic and possibility consciousness in our leadership tool kit. Magnetism has power inherent in it, but it is a power used to unify, not separate or isolate, and power to support a quality of appropriate love in our leadership actions. A good definition of magnetism would include a unique balance of power and love.

If there is a caution with this competency of Magnetism, it is a concern that Magnetism not be used as manipulation to achieve personal egoic aims and cause harm to others. Magnetism helps us establish nourishing relationships and our genuine warm-heartedness with others allows us to build teams, organizations and tribes that care for each other and the whole. The competency of Magnetism moves us into the paradigm of collective intelligence and gives us a direct perception that the whole is greater than the sum of the parts.

Competency Four: Uncreate/Destroy *(other words to describe are: Let Go, Cut, Release, Uncreate, Endings)*

This competency directs us to face into endings, completions, and impermanence. Our question becomes: "What is dying, or needs to die, so that the new can be born?" With practice, we become more able to sense the subtlety of situations. Our timing is crisp. We know when to let go so that the new can come in.

The fourth competency encourages us to grow our capacity to know when situations are complete—when it is time to let go and allow something new to emerge. This skill requires an ability to remember the truth of impermanence and the lived experience of the cycles of birth and death in all things. The practice of this competency strengthens the leader's willingness to operate from a place of wisdom and freedom that is beyond his or her personal preferences. The useful question is always: "What is dying, or needs to die?" Only when this process is welcomed, can we make space for what wants to be born. Two impulses can occur with this competency: a) to act impulsively, and prematurely 'destroy or let go'. b) to hold on too long, refusing to act, being unwilling to cut and uncreate.

With practice, we become more able to perceive the subtle nature of situations and our timing choice is clear: we know exactly when to let go of one reality and welcome another.

Competency Five: Spaciousness *(other words to describe are: Seeing Through Solidity, Openness and All Possibilities, Hidden Potential, Soul-Inspired)*

This competency invites us to see through the solidity of things—how they appear—and perceive directly the true nature of whatever is appearing. Spaciousness can operate as a separate competency or be a part of each of the other competencies. Strengthened by meditation practice, this competency is experienced as a deep knowing and/or strong intuition, often arising from the body.

The fifth competency may be present in all the other competencies, or operate as a single, separate competency. This skill has a direct connection to a heart-based focus and is strengthened by cultivating some form of meditation/mindfulness practice. With time and practice, we develop the ability to perceive the difference between how things appear, i.e. show up, and how they really are. Some may call this 'strong intuition' and that seems appropriate. If we can see through the surface confusion of any situation, and see into the deeper meaning of what is occurring, we allow the spacious quality of our own awareness to be a healing force for whatever is dying and whatever is being born. At this point, our presence is the only and highest leadership action we can offer.

When these competencies are present within the leader, at all stages of development and levels of scale, we can live in basic goodness and partner with the living systems that serve life. We enter into deep partnership with the sacred. We experience the true value of being human and offer our gifts without holding back.

Practice: Explore a personal relationship to the 5 friends.

On paper, finish the following sentences:
   a. I feel safe when...
   b. I feel supported when...
   c. I feel free when... I feel creative when...
   d. When I speak my truth, I feel...
   e. I feel valued when...

Choose a work or leadership situation and identify which of the 5 friends are present, and which are absent. What action(s) can you take to make the situation more open, nourishing, and creative? Do the same process with a significant relationship.

Reflection questions:

1. Imagine how your work and world would be altered if you were able to utilize the Peace Making Competency with ease.
2. Recall a time when listening to all voices resulted in a greater sense of wholeness and new possibility by Enrichment.
3. How would you evaluate your capacity to Magnetize in your role(s) as leader? What would be the impact if you knew how to use Magnetizing skillfully? Consider how your own leadership would change if you focused on magnetizing your people.
4. How might the fourth competency of uncreate/destroy help you simplify your life? Would knowing how to 'let go' bring more grace and flow to your leadership style?
5. How might the competency of spaciousness build your self-confidence and willingness to take risks, based on your own inner knowing?

Neuroscience

I'm doing my work in the world because the Karma
needs a scientific platform to be received.
- Richie Davidson

I t's natural to wonder who we are and how we fit into the universe.
Science, spirituality, religion, self-study, parenting, history, and nature
can all provide means of figuring out our place in the grand story of life
on Earth. Each form of inquiry provides a useful entry point, but our
understanding is strengthened with diverse perspectives. Magic happens
when we can combine our objective and subjective inquiries together.
Science alone without practical application and human usefulness is
flat, while human spirituality without science isn't embodied in the
21st century. Both can become oppressive and aggressive when taken
as the only way to understand truth. Together, they are more than the
sum of both parts.

Science can provide grounding roots for our imagination of who
we are in the universe. It can be an entry point for those skeptical
of meditation and inner exploration, or for those who see safety and
connection as 'soft'. Neuroscience can be a way to meet people where
they are. The logical can be a gateway to the heart.

With science, our collective sense of spirit and self can reach
new heights. Current neuroscience provides greater awareness of our

subjective experience. It provides validation for what's going on inside of us. The more we know about ourselves, the more powerful we are.

The real purpose of neuroscience is validation. Neuroscience establishes and gives us validation for our subjective experience. The only way out of suffering is to increase awareness, which gives us freedom of choice. In basic terms: neuroscience has established that human beings will respond with compassion and empathy, and love and care, if there is not threat or trauma in their environment. This gift of establishing safety through awareness allows our basic goodness to flow uninhibited.

We include neuroscience to give people a glimpse of what is going on inside of them, and to show how it applies to the level of the group. The more we know about ourselves, and how we're meant to function, the more we can work with ourselves individually and collectively. MatrixWorks makes scientific study useful to group and individual relationships. Neuroscience is another lens to look inside, giving access to our inner and relational experience.

The latest neuroscience offers fresh and exciting perspectives on group behavior. As we are finding, our neurosystems are deeply connected to the inner systems of the people around us, creating an interwoven web of connection amongst individuals and groups. While we may have a ways to go before experiencing this inner intimacy, we can surely move away from the concept of isolation. We are not isolated beings. Our genius depends upon our ability to connect; In fact, our very survival depends upon it. We feel those around us and they feel us. Therefore, group life has a profound impact upon our inner states, and our inner states have a profound impact on group life. The implications of these findings urge us to nurture our emotional lives and foster healthy connections. We see every individual as essential and inclusion as our primary purpose in groups. Creativity cannot happen without it. Deepening into our felt senses can help us emerge as spontaneous, growing, interpersonal individuals and organizations.

Neuroscience research challenges the predominant cultural ideas of competition and survival of the fittest. We can no longer view man as nasty and brutish. In fact, humans have a strong capacity for connection, "we instinctively become more attentive to the faces around us, searching for smiles or frowns that give us a better sense of how to interpret signs of danger or that might signal someone's intentions" (Goleman, 2006, p. 38). Since humans interpret their immediate environments through a group process, it is important in group work to attend to the feeling of safety. Intentionality matters, and we as groups want to feel connected through mutual goals and direction. If we detect that the inner state and the outer movements are out of sync, we will put up our defense mechanisms that block us from our own creativity and genius.

Beyond safety, we want to feel free to creatively and authentically express ourselves. Every person is the hero of their own story, and our lives and work are grounds in which to explore our expression and self-emergence. If we are to create healthy group environments, our groups may provide us these same qualities in which to grow and flourish. Groups can be a place where we happily participate for the sake of mutual evolution. To find these sorts of healthy group environments, we must attend to providing evolutionary conditions (for example: basic goodness, living systems, 5 friends) as well. We must pay attention to the impact we have on the group as a whole, because we become important to its overall health and function. Ultimately, it is us who choose whether our felt worlds resemble a natural garden or a competitive arena.

We offer these studies as a bridge to turn theory into practice that can make a difference in our lives. It turns the case for a relational world into hard science. The power of integrating the subjective experience with the scientific exploration has the best chance of supporting change. If it's just my experience, doubt can come in; if it's just scientific it can be cold and a little mechanical. If they align together then there's a shift in my identity that can change my experience in groups.

We also encourage participants to undergo a scientific exploration of their own experience, gathering data from their relationships and what makes them thrive in groups, and experimenting with different ways of knowing and different ways of practicing relationships. Buddha's last words were "be a lamp for yourself. Don't believe what I say. Work out your own salvation with diligence."

The following are the common frameworks we borrow from Neuroscience and apply to our group work:

Social Engagement System

> *"We are impressed by mounting scientific evidence suggesting that, in two basic ways, the human child is hardwired to connect. First, we are hardwired to connect to other people. Second, we are hardwired to connect to moral meaning and to the possibility of the transcendent. Meeting these basic needs for connectedness is essential to health and to human flourishing." (from HARDWIRED TO CONNECT: The New Scientific Case for Authoritative Communities)*

Dr. Stephen Porges developed the Traffic Light Metaphor for the human nervous system. Humans have evolved a "Smart Part" of our nervous system. The vagus nerve is the nerve of compassion—and it is the body's caretaking organ. The vagus nerve evolved to support bonding between humans. Centered in the face and head, the vagus nerve is influenced by connection, especially in face-to-face contact. It is connected to a rich network of oxytocin receptors, the hormone associated with love and trust (oxytocin is the hormone released in the body to stimulate maternal bonding during childbirth, and it can also be activated by eleven seconds of eye contact or a twenty-second hug). By understanding the workings of the vagus nerve and oxytocin, we can consciously choose to bring love and safety into our group experiences.

We have learned to use connection to establish safety for ourselves (the green zone). In the green zone, we have the power of choice, because we feel safe in relationship. If we can't establish safety through connection, then only fight, flight or freeze reactions are available to us (the yellow zone). If we are in danger then we go into the red zone, where only freeze is available. In groups, we don't want to be reactive all the time, we want to feel safe enough to discover the choice of mutual creation.

Practice: The metaphor of safety

Allow yourself to remember all the people who have helped you become who you are, who taught you about connection: Parents, Teachers, Work and Life Partners, Mentors. Let yourself recall the kindness and good will and care you have received. Feel a long line of people behind you, supporting you. Let yourself know how you have been there for others. Allow yourself to recognize your great good fortune to be who you are and where you are in this moment. Feel once again that second intelligence, already completed and preserved inside you. A freshness in the center of the chest. A second knowing that moves from within you, a fountainhead, moving out.

Reflection: where are you Tracking Green, Yellow, and Red in yourself, your teams and organizations?

Limbic Brain

Located within the central part of the brain, in between the neocortex (responsible for executive function) and the amygdala (responsible for survival functions) is our limbic brain. The limbic brain regulates emotions, behaviors, and motivation. It is unique to mammals; it's how we bond, care for our young, and care for each other. Through this brain we 'feel' for each other, and engage in learning through play, nurture, and communication.

The limbic brain is the essential regulatory center between higher reasoning and survival instinct. In our modern culture and workplace, executive function is highly prized. It is responsible for the ability to think critically, make decisions, decipher ethics, coordinate thoughts with actions, and moderate social behaviors. However, we don't always give priority to this part of the brain, because when we sense a threat in our environment (whether physical, or social, or emotional), the amygdala 'hijacks' the attention in the brain and sends us into survival mode. In survival mode, the only options available to us are fight, flight, freeze, or appease. The limbic system allows us to recover from what the brain experiences as a triggering threat when the amygdala has taken over. So, when we're emotionally reactive or want to engage our higher executive functions, the best solution is to engage in safe connection with others. By engaging the limbic system through safe connection (eye contact, deep listening, openness, a hug, an authentic compliment) with another, we can recover the neocortex and our ability to think clearly. This understanding of the brain gives us permission to bring love and relationship into groups as essential tools for accomplishing more, together.

Mirror Neurons

These were discovered in monkeys 20 years ago. Mirror neurons are neurons that fire both when an animal acts, and when the animal observes the action in another. Marco Iacoboni more recently discovered mirror neurons in humans. These explain what's happening in the brain when we feel empathy, understanding, and resonance. Mirror neurons explain how we can walk into a room and suddenly feel different, knowing how others in that room are feeling. We're naturally drawn towards paying attention to other beings, because we experience what's happening for others in ourselves. Imagine what's possible when we acknowledge this truth in our workplaces, instead of denying and ignoring it.

In groups, where we experience the emotions of other members, it is important to differentiate and support. Not every emotion or problem belongs to us. We get to experiment with the question: "does this belong to me?" If I'm in a process group and someone is being stuck, I can ask whether it is my experience or whether I am responding to the other person's experience. I have been influenced through the constructions in my brain with the person who is having the experience and I am responding as though it belongs to me, even through it doesn't. And if it is not mine, how do I stay connected and simultaneously release it so that I can self-regulate.

Empathic attunement is the feeling of being felt by others. It is the way we feel connected and essential to group genius. It is the emotional resonance that creates coupled harmony between individuals in groups. This sense of emotional balance fuels the system to move forward. We can detect systems drivers in the field simply by watching and trusting what our bodies are indicating to us. Mirror neurons help us sense the emotions of other people by mimicking their internal state within our brains and bodies. Since our limbic systems resonate with one another, it is in our own best interest as individuals and as groups to heal one another. In fact, it is in our very DNA to embrace loving connections for our survival, "nature tends to foster positive relationships" (Goleman, 2006, p. 44).

Practice: Bring your awareness to a time when you felt somewhat dis-regulated or agitated. Even better if you can become aware of your feelings in the moment. Then, ask yourself the question: "Is this about me? Or have I been influenced by something seen by my mirror neurons?" Pay attention to the subtle differenced between your own feelings and when you're taking on the feelings of others. Reflect on how you can reset your nervous system back to center. Practice this with positive emotions: find someone celebrating, laughing, holding hands, and see if you can make space to experience their love and joy affecting you.

Influence on Group Dynamics

Information supports transformation; giving knowledge about neuroscience is empowering. Neuroscience theories provide structure, but they aren't the energy. They just spark the energy to flow, and we can only trust that the right process will arise.

Across all borders and boundaries, all cultures and races, all religions and politics, humans are universally motivated by happiness and connection. This is good news for shifting group behavior and relationships. If we understand our own happiness as connected to the happiness of our neighbor, we might engage in behaviors that foster mutual social kindness.

4 Pillars
The Code for Living Systems

Our subjective experience is the essential complement to an understanding of neuroscience. If science gives us an outer cognitive awareness, the four pillars offer us an inner intuitive awareness. We can strengthen our self-awareness through the four pillars of the inner world:

- Somatic wisdom and intelligence of the body
- Subtle energy
- Mindfulness and relational field awareness
- Interconnectedness

The four pillars are like the DNA pattern for each group. They serve as the basic architecture pattern that provides structure for becoming aware of our subjective experience. They reference how we give and receive energy and information. They help us move towards health. The following chapters investigate each of these four pillars in more depth.

Continually paying attention to these four pillars would result in working in a living systems way. Orienting towards living systems as guardrails, group systems will become brilliant in nature when continually applied. While you could add more elements, you can't remove any of these and still have something that's life affirming. Contrasted to an orientation of extracting everything we can from the living world and from other people, these four pillars provide us a new orientation from which to build a new living world. If you're practicing these, you are doing living, sustainable, work.

Somatic Wisdom
Wisdom and intelligence of the body

"Health is the integration of differentiated parts"
-Dan Siegel, M.D.

T rusting the wisdom and intelligence of the body allows us to use the body as a tool of consciousness; the information that I receive from my body is informing my consciousness. Psychology often refers to the body as the unconscious mind, and this leads us to make a distinction of what we mean by body. There is the body of flesh and form, and the body of energy and awareness. How they support each other is a gift in leaning into and trusting intuition available in the body. The body does speak its mind. Learning how to trust your own experience of information coming from your body is an important step in working in a living way. Learning how to see information in the body of the group and in the bodies of the people who are members of the group helps to plan interventions in the group that are most useful, relevant, and on the mark. Our bodies tell the truth, and unleashing the energy stored in the body moves people and groups towards healing and creativity.

One of the clear ways that we make use of the body in this work is through the body systems. Our bodies are the most immediate and intimate Living System we have contact with. Within our bodies are parts within parts, systems within systems that are whole in themselves and also make up larger wholes. I've had success bringing these into organizations, helping teams reference the group as a body and the body

28

as a group. As a metaphor, the body can teach us a lot about diversity, communication and the many paradoxes of the "parts and the whole" (often referred to as 'holons'). Our bodies need all parts to belong to the whole and to fulfill their own unique functions and tasks, which is not unlike how teams need to function: each person fulfilling their specific responsibilities, yet participating in the processes of the whole.

There's been a series of research studies tracking the role of oxytocin that women have more of, and what this hormone predisposes us to do in stress. People with high levels of oxytocin will tend and befriend during stress. They will reach out rather than drop out. If this hormone is lacking in the body, then we will isolate, disconnect, disappear, or go into a metaphorical cave. Knowing this as a facilitator can influence how I intervene in a group and can inform me about what to track for as I'm learning how to facilitate a group as a living system. *Note about oxytocin: a twenty second hug, or twelve seconds of eye contact, releases oxytocin in the body and in general it's one of natures antidepressants and anti-anxiety sources. So the body is the most creative event that's ever happened! It would take thousands of computers to match all the things that the human brain does all on its own. We are constantly referencing the knowing-ness that comes from our bodies.*

Through our willingness to learn from the body, we can discover how to use differing and varied kinds of intelligence, perception and consciousness represented by different members of our teams in our human organizations. In other words, by becoming students of the systems of the body, we can gain skill in working with creativity, differences and diversity. These are skills we need to make our teams, groups, and organizations more healthy and capable of responding to the demands of our times. The body represents 650 million years of evolutionary wisdom and history. As such, the Body-as-Resource deserves to be included in our explorations of how to create life affirming human systems and organizations.

The following suggestions about the wisdoms and intelligences of the systems have been derived from on-going personal study and training with Susan Aposhan, author of *Natural Intelligence*. I have developed the following template for using the body metaphor to help groups and teams function more like a living body:

- Wisdom of the bones and joints, "the ancient ones": represent support and structure, groundedness, clarity and objectivity, neutrality. Attend to structure, non-emotional, neutral, grounding
- Wisdom of the muscles and connective tissue, "doers and builders": physical vitality, strength, power, task, purpose, likes to 'push against' in a positive way. Focus on tasks, on getting the job done, likes 'push'
- Wisdom of the organs, "the hearth of the home": slow, deep and true, processing, digesting and transforming, at home with "need", at home with emotion. Loves processing, attends to deeper needs, slower
- Wisdom of the endocrine system, "spice of life"; "spurts/burst of energy": growth, metabolism, overall energy level, interested in subtle energy, connected to the chakra system, changeable, mercurial. Emotional, energetic, changeable
- Wisdom of the brain and Central nervous system, "major coordination, processing, and control center of body": organizer, director, watcher, and gives alertness and problem-solving ability. Problem-solving, director, organizer, "CEO". 3 Levels to autonomic nervous system:
  a) para-sympathetic -- most primitive, rest, relaxation
  b) sympathetic -- mobilization, fight or flight
  c) socially engaged -- "smart nervous system" assesses safety, trust, bonding and love. Concerned with relationship and connection between human beings. Most evolved part of human system.
- Wisdom of the fluids, "Mother" "Caregiver": sense of flow, yielding, capacity to let go, spaciousness, timelessness, presence, transportation of information molecules and neuropeptides which comprise 98% of communication in the body. Prefers a 'flow', soft and mothering, connecting

- Wisdom of the breath, "foundation of life": links inner and outer, links body and mind, moves us into sensation, enables us to access the wisdom of each system. Life force, sees the whole
- Wisdom of cellular consciousness, "fearless confidence": devotion, egolessness, ability to transform, become whatever is needed, commitment to the whole, willing to sacrifice. Willing to play any part

The body wouldn't function without each of these parts working in harmony. I invite each member to choose a body system to play out a role in conducting a project. Then they complete the project using the wisdom of their part. This helps group members work with differences as gifts, while seeing that all parts are necessary for the health of the whole body system. Then, we apply this learning to the part they play in their group.

The whole/part relationship, called "holons" by systems thinkers, seems to be a key pattern of organization of the body. A holon expresses similarity at the level of the part and the whole. These holons express both autonomy and interdependence. They are able to respond, protect, defend, and support life, acting with an intelligence and creativity that is beyond the capacity of 6400 computers all linked together. Candice Pert, PhD., Neuroscientific Researcher and author of Molecules of Emotion says, "The mind is in every cell of the body... intelligence flows throughout the system, happening all over, all at once." What this means for us is that we can look to the body as both a metaphor and reality for how living systems distribute intelligence throughout all parts of its system.

I often used this practice in my work in corporate settings, with much success. The fullness of my work in the corporate world was from 1999 through 2012. One group in particular sticks out as an example of using the work to improve their process and efficiency. During that time the work I was doing was cutting edge, and now it's become more mainstream. But when I think back to when I started, there were two or three main issues or blocks to groups having access to a deeper capacity for collective intelligence: structures that inhibited creative flow, taking things too seriously, and the mistake of telling people what they need instead of deep listening and relating.

I worked with the girl's toy division at Mattel, traveling almost once a month from 1999 to 2003 to consult with all the people making dolls. One of the significant things I introduced to them was the body systems. I would create exercises that gave them permission to reveal their full selves, risk trusting each other, and risk believing something else is possible. I introduced the exercise by explaining the body intelligences (listed above) and that the body is the most creative thing that's ever happened in the universe, and if they wanted to become more creative we could use the body as a metaphor.

Their task was to re-imagine how products were designed and created. At the time, their product creation process was painful and exhausting. They would create a doll and follow it all the way through the design process, only to be criticized and chopped to pieces at the end of the line. That form of criticism wasn't helping this team's creative juices.

Our task was to redesign how the creation to execution product process happened. One of those teams came up with the idea of staying in their body system role, which revamped how this process was happening. They identified what was happening now, what wisdoms had dominance, and which ones were being left out. Then they designed a new process that integrated all the systems, by looking at how flow and structure could work together.

The process changed by starting to hold peer reviews, and holding an open meeting for appreciative feedback from the team at different intervals in the production line. They created an internal system of intermittent critiques, had prototypes made in china, and then held a final review. Through prototyping and feedback, gnarly issues had been cleared up, so the changes weren't so catastrophic for the designers. The touchstones helped concerns and issues get resolved earlier in the process, which quickly sped up the process. I was astonished. The team totally changed everything for the production of girl's dolls. They were accomplishing the same workload, with more innovative creations, within cycles of eight to twelve *weeks*, in product cycles that took others eighteen to twenty-four *months* to accomplish.

Teaching this increased level of vitality unleashed the creative impulse of the body. The design group was able to tap into and learn from the body's wisdom. The power of the body partnered with this group to produce success. Looking at nature can give us ideas about how health can be in systems. We can learn from the body about how to create health at the level of the group, because the body is a group and the group is a body.

Practice: Wisdom of the Body

We all have all parts, yet some may be more obvious in each of us. Use the parts of the body (above) to identify who brings what competencies to your group. Have each member try on a "role" in the body, and perform a task from that perspective. This model can be used to give appreciative feedback to each other.

Subtle Energy
The role of subtle energy in the body of groups

"Emotions are the music of the mind" --Daniel Siegel

S tructure and energy are the powerful two sides of a coin in understanding group dynamics. As we saw in the prior section about the structures in the body, healthy structures can produce great creativity (while rigid structures will create blockages). When structure and energy are not aligned in a group, the birth of a new possibility can't really happen.

Subtle energy is the secret magic that flows through a group. Focusing on this phenomenon can help us track the unseen forces that guide a group or relationship towards health. Emotions can be an entry point to tracking the subtle movements of energy within the body, between people, and among the field of the group. Ancient healing traditions of many cultures and practices recognize and work with subtle energy, though our modern scientific study has been slow to 'verify' these wisdoms. One of the ways that our technology serves us is that we're more able to measure higher levels of subtle energy. For example, the work Heart Math Institute has accomplished in measuring the subtle energy field around the heart and the brain. Scientific validation offers us permission to include this as a part of our field of awareness. Subtle energy is where we begin to differentiate objective data with our subjective experience, and validate each person's feelings, especially if they are different from our own. If we're using our own bodies and feelings as an instrument of consciousness, then we want to be able to sense subtle energies, what they are, and to identify the qualities of this subtle energy.

Metaphors are a real gift in being able to work with the subtle energies in groups. Metaphors that have meaning for groups help reveal roles people play and provide understanding of different leadership styles. Metaphors can help groups diagnose when they are out of balance and when they are in balance and creative flow. Chakras, elements, ecosystems, body organs, and seasons can all serve as metaphors for a group understanding the energy that runs through the group structures.

How I bring mindfulness into business

Early on, a team renamed my use of "a moment of mindfulness" to "the power of 2 minutes." I loved that they changed it to something that worked for them. It was so typically business oriented. The framing that made sense to them was: "we're slowing down now in order to go faster later." No matter what you call it, we are helping people through mindfulness to shift their consciousness[3] into direct awareness to different levels of perception. Mindfulness practice helps people discover the practical value of being self aware, receptive to others, and to learn to listen to the whisper of what wants to happen. The commitment of normalizing mindfulness into companies supports ongoing organizational intelligence and learning.

Practice: Resourcing Self for Subtle Energy

The following are suggestions on how to facilitate and ignite the genius of any group through your MatrixWorks Group Facilitation. These are tips for how to resource yourself before energetically engaging the group.

35

Step 1: Drop into experiencing and feeling your body, aware of how energy is flowing in your body. Take as long as you need. You can be general in your focus, or very specific. For example: How does my skin feel? What about my Bones? What about my Fluids, organs etc.? Doing this at the beginning of facilitation allows for the Facilitator's inner competence to bring about coherence in the group.

Step one is intended to bring attention and awareness into your body as a base/ground to stabilize the energy. Our body is one of the most important sources of wisdom and intuition in Groups.

Step 2: Imagine that you can really feel and connect with the midline of your body (the spine, the central channel, whatever name resonates with you). The capacity to be in a state of neutrality is engendered by focusing on the midline. This midline is connected to our sense of will – which is something we can clarify by having an intention for the goodness of the group, the right action of the group, the best for everyone in the group. Applying the midline gathers your energy and brings it under your own direction. Unconscious intentions can drive our behavior and lead to disorder. Holding a will for healing will make this part of your consciousness before you even begin to interact with the group. It sets the field of the group.

Step 3: Next, check in with your emotional orientation in the moment: 'How am I feeling?' What tells me I'm okay just now?' 'What lets me know I'm safe?' Resource your emotional presence, and after spending a few moments on that, you'd want to do the same thing with your sense of the quality of your mind. Of course, this is a lot of focus and preparation of oneself before stepping into leadership, but this is a sequence that can empower you to become much more effective in how you interact with the group. You build your foundation before moving into action.

All of the preparation is good practice in mindfulness and self-awareness, essential skills for conscious Leaders.

Reflection: In your relationships, groups, and work, do structures (rules, habits, processes, buildings, etc.) support the free flow of energy (creativity, love, and emotions), and does the free flow of energy strengthen the structures? Are there any guiding metaphors that offer you permission to experience subtle energy in your life?

Relational Field
Mindfulness and Relational Field Awareness

Nothing is itself without everything else.
- Brian Swimme

When you put these intelligences of structure in the body and subtle energy together, there's a cross-pollination. We start to become aware of the subtle ways in which we are interconnected with each other and the larger whole. This awareness may not always be available to us in our every day lives (perhaps you've touched it from time to time), but when we put intention into becoming aware of interconnectedness, we tap into a universal energy that connects us with all that is.

Nothing exists in isolation, and at the fundamental atomic level, everything is connected. Yet when we live in such isolated bubbles, how do we begin to see ourselves as part of everything else? How do we begin to live in a way that reflects our connection to all beings? Paying attention to relationships helps us move beyond the concept of interconnection into the direct perception and felt experience of interconnectedness. If we can have that experience, then we can perceive the whole as greater than the sum as its parts, and the whole in every part. Oftentimes we focus too deeply on a part, and miss the essence of the whole. We can remind ourselves not to mistake the part for the whole in relationships. Problems arise when we follow our thinking instead of following the patterns of how nature works.

When we have a direct perception of interconnectedness, the four immeasurables (Buddhist virtues of loving kindness, joy, compassion, and balance that are the antidote to negativity) arise and are inherent. The four immeasurables are boundless states, they have no limit and are "beyond measure." They are qualities that arise from our original nature. According to the Tibetan tradition, we human beings are connate (meaning born together) with these qualities. They hold the place of being the most universal and most personal. Because of this, the possibility of healing our human wounds through reconnecting to these qualities is immediate. We could say the four immeasurables are the lap of the mother we can crawl into for loving safety.

It is our assumption and experience in the MatrixWorks model of working with Groups as Living Systems that these qualities are the doorway to and fruit of the consciousness phase of a group's life. Genuine cultivation of these qualities invites mutual connection, and the experience of creative evolution will contain these qualities. It is a two-way street, for sure.

At this stage of a group's life, we have the possibility to re-encounter a matrix of connection and bond more deeply with our true nature and each other. In this state, the truth of non-separateness is available as a direct experience. Once the immeasurables are experienced, mutual connection joins with the transpersonal and we are moved toward greater wholeness of being.

In the early days of MatrixWorks, there was not much research about the results our work produced, although leaders felt more comfortable leading teams where intelligence was distributed, and people were bringing their unique gifts to the workplace.

These results from the research conducted on productivity were the benefit of teams building skills in three levels: tools to help team members connect to themselves, tools to help team members connect to one another, and tools to help team members connect to their task. Connection is a fundamental human need, and yet in many organizations it is not understood to be essential for accomplishing task. It is seen as something you did in the healing world, but not in business. MatrixWorks proved that if you want to really innovate, you cannot skip this part. I made this more palatable by linking the concepts of connection to current neuroscience and understanding of brain psychology. I led with science and linked it to how it could help teams be more productive. Because that's the first thing I do in every group: build a lot of safety so that people can drop their defenses and become receptive to the energy of flow.

Practice: Be a welcoming

Stand with a partner and beam/radiate to them that they're welcome here. Then, travel from person to person, offering this welcoming beam. Open your heart to receiving the welcoming from others. Then imagine every member connected to every other member, woven in a matrix of goodness.

Helping people to feel safe through welcoming does a lot to lower the noise (of interpersonal incoherence and confusion). When coherent resonance comes through, we can rest in a field of safety in groups.

Reflection: Choose an evolutionary partner-someone to reflect which of the following statements is true or false. Are any of these blind spots for you? Are any of these competencies of yours?

Key competencies about groups as living systems:
- The whole is greater then the sum of its parts.
- Intelligence is distributed throughout the system.
- Wisdom/answers unfold from within.
- Capacity to self-organize; self generate; self correct; and self regulate.
- Groups cannot be controlled.

- Groups can only be contained or perturbed.
- Use messes and mistakes to move towards order and coherence.
- Alternates between chaos and order.
- Thrives on feedback.
- If you cut it in half you do not end up with two.
- Seek relations, connection that leads to more complex systems and relationships. (Atoms to molecules, molecules to cells, cells to tissue, tissue to organs, organs to larger bodies, humans to each other, to families, to tribes, to work organizations, etc.).

Field Awareness
Interconnectedness and Field Awareness

*Everything that irritates us about others can lead
us to an understanding of ourselves.*
- Carl Jung

We know fields when we walk into a room and have a feeling or gut sense of what's going on. We even create fields with our own energy and when our energy mixes with others. Consciously or subconsciously, our brains are paying attention to the safety level in a field. I'm always tracking the field, trying to see the invisible. Individuals and their interactions give us early indications of the invisible field. The field that's created in MatrixWorks has a quality of intimacy that is deeply nourishing. We can walk into fields, and we can create them. The field we're creating is such that we can heal our traumas and not act out our traumas.

MatrixWorks moves the focus from the potency of a charismatic leader towards discovering the potency of the field. When each member is empowered and working in right relationship with each other, then the field is fully potent, and creative emergence seems to happen by itself. The relational field can speak through you, through a synergistic partner, and even through the wind blowing outside. Moving awareness from the individual person to the field invokes much more communication with the invisible realms.

One of the most fascinating phenomena, especially in teaching

MatrixWorks in communities over a period of time (specifically in the United States, Brazil and Japan), is the continuation of themes from group to group. We do a training and the group achieves a certain level of consciousness, and the next group seems to start where the last group left off. This really makes me think there's some kind of evolutionary process across the fields of groups. Consciousness allows this movement towards more capacity and more coherence become apparent in group life.

I even saw it in corporations, in trainings months apart and from different teams. The field you create in one group affects the consciousness of the next. It is the universe's evidence that healing is working through a quality of harmony that ripples out into the world.

People often ask me whether compassion in the business world dulls the competitive edge. What I've found is that when companies start to work with interconnectedness, an energetic shift from competition to common intention happens. In my trainings, I introduce a practice about helping your partner shine, which brings emphasis to this shift. The simple but powerful practice has people share in pairs and then with the whole group:

1. Something they want or need *from* the other person as they work together.
2. Something they want *for* the other person as they partner on the project.

Setting these intentions at the get-go is a way of balancing the giving and receiving of the relational field. It subtly shifts the energy from "what can I get" into a dynamic balance that gives energy and sustainability to a creative group. It builds the experience of interconnectedness. In a co-learning and co-presencing environment, the focus is on relationship rather than one person being the star.

Practice: Pay attention to how you are feeling when you enter a room of people. If you're feeling a certain way, do you notice that others in the room seem to resonate with your feelings? Do you pick up on what's already circulating in the room as much as your energy affects the field? Experiment with projecting your positive intentions into groups, and notice what happens.

Essential Patterns

Group life flows in patterns. Sometimes it moves like the beat of the breath, and sometimes it follows a broken record. MatrixWorks has found that healthy, functioning groups follow the golden ratio pattern. This means finding a balance somewhere in between two polarities.

Neuroscience, inner work, living systems, and basic goodness have provided our basic teaching frameworks, and now we transition into teaching the group about how healthy group behavior moves. We move from self-awareness to group and relationship awareness. When the ground is steady and strong, transformation emerges from this fertile ground.

When facilitating transformation, it can be tempting to try to accomplish healing all at once. Remembering these essential patterns helps the facilitator and the group remember the paradox that we are perfect already as we are, and there is also still room for improvement. Focusing our awareness on dynamic patterns, demonstrated in the following chapters, helps groups find balance in creative evolution.

Three is a powerful number. The triangle is the strongest form in the universe, and we see this represented throughout our work. When we work in themes of three, what starts as a basic pattern takes on a life of its own and continues to grow and evolve. I've always been interested in fractals, in the various shapes that represent infinite emergence. I began to understand it as a living geometry, a way of seeing the natural world. Fractals are an example of how patterns are repeated. Mandel Broad discovered that the simplest equation, repeated again and again into a computer, would produce the most complex fractal patterns.

45

Fractals represent the basic pattern between living systems and organizations. They point to the self-similarity that's present in anything living; that what's true at the smallest level is also true at every level of scale. A small piece of a cauliflower, or tree branch, or a shell will hold the same pattern as the larger system. A small department will represent the truth of a whole organization. Any change to a part will send ripples out into the whole.

Fractals remind us of the truth of the whole and parts. The hypothesis I've worked with is that the fractal equation of MatrixWorks is the simple equation of inclusion and connection, conflict and chaos, and creative evolution and consciousness. You'll find many sets of three throughout the book, and these are always healthful starting points for generating fractal energy. When applied to life and the unfolding of groups, we see patterns of health and life become more complex. To become a living system the group has to continuously go through this simple equation.

In my work and in the work of MatrixWorks, we see this phenomenon with self-similarity at different levels of scale (from the personal, to the relational, to the team, to the organization, to the world). Because they are associated with a living geometry, fractals help us in how we see the group. Find the formulas that work for you and see what happens when you continually iterate and repeat that intervention in your group. In MatrixWorks, we work with an abundance of threes that unleash life-affirming fractal group patterns. Because the threes are constantly spiraling and shifting, it adds a degree of complexity to working with groups, and it's not always easy to learn to track these components. Ultimately the complexity of tracking these stages, levels, and capacities forces our mind to shift (or perhaps we should say relax) to a broader, more inclusive, holistic view. Here are a few examples:

- 3 stages of group life: connection, chaos or conflict, and creative evolution and consciousness
- 3 levels of connection: intra-personal connection, interpersonal connection, field connection
- 3 functions of a group: accomplish task, attend to relationships, nourish members
- 3 parts of the brain: reptilian, mammalian, neocortex
- 3 aspects of being: inner, outer, secret

In a living systems model, there is a dominant pattern that makes anything living more dynamic. When we try to apply a new model of health, the pattern of thesis, antithesis, and synthesis arises. There is always a time for pause or awkward growth during the integration of something new.

Intra, Inter, Field
The Three Levels of Connection

MatrixWorks provides a subtle energy approach to facilitation–constantly tracking what's going on inside ourselves, between people, and within the group as a whole. Paying attention to these three levels provides an exciting new approach that encourages us to see the group as a living system/living being. Seeing the Group as a Living System, makes new possibilities available to us. We experience a sense of belonging and intimacy, balanced with an experience of our uniqueness and autonomy. Being able to feel both our belonging and intimacy, as well as our autonomy and uniqueness is one of the genuine longings of the 21st century.

A healthy group attends to all three of these levels of relating at once:

Intrapersonal: This means the interior experience of each member. Are we tracking each individual and the impact that the group is having on them? It is essential to remember that it is not important to be right about what is happening for them, or to make a clever interpretation, it is only important that you demonstrate that you care about what is happening for them.

Interpersonal: This means tracking the connections between members. Who is connected to whom? Is there anyone in the group that is not connected? Are there unnamed special relationships? Are the members with special relationships sharing their love with the larger whole or are they forming a clique? How can I help people connect to each other?

The Field: On one level this refers to the energy and personality of the group as a whole. What are the shared themes arising? What is the unique energy of this group? What are the emergent properties arising from all these individuals coming together? On another, more intuitive level, the field has a distinctly transpersonal feel, as though these members have conspired to be together for reasons that none of us can know, we can only discover and uncover.

Learning to facilitate in this way will help us to create more and more groups that function as healthy Living Systems. Through this art, we create a more living and loving world. We know we belong and we are unique.

Practice: The Goodness Exercise

Feeling your uniqueness, allow yourself to remember all the people who have helped you become who you are. Bring to your awareness all the people who taught you about Love, about Leadership, Connection, Safety, Support, Freedom, Truth, Value and Worth, how to be in Relationship. Remember the goodness of your Parents, Teachers, Work and Life Partners, Mentors. Let yourself recall the kindness and good will and care you have received. Feel a long line of people behind you, supporting you. The lineages you are apart of. The cells within you. Let yourself know how you have been there for others. Allow yourself to recognize your great good fortune to be who you are and where you are in this moment. Appreciate that you are welcome here. You are safe. The loneliness is over. You are a part of the web of life from which you can not fall. You are an intrinsic part of the relational field of all life. You are called to make a new world where relationship is valued, where Love and Leadership go together. You are here because you have answered this call. You know we are here to Love.

Capacities of a Group
The Three Functions of a Healthy Group

Research from MIT and Stanford say High-Performing Groups and Leaders do three things continuously and consistently: Accomplish Tasks, Attend to Relationship, Cultivate cultures of Well-Being and Nourishment. Here's the formula for success:

Accomplish Task: Can the group accomplish its task? What would help the group accomplish its task?

Nourish the Members: Does this group know how to nurture one another or have they created an environment in which spending time together is depleting? Is their love to share in this group? How can we create nourishment for this group?

Attend to Relationship: Can this group accomplish its task without ignoring the feelings and contributions of each member? Does the group pit task against process or can they accomplish a task and still make time to process the feelings of the members?

Another complementary lens we use is: **Being, Doing, and Relating.** Being is the aspect of essence. Doing is more about skills, or actions, or direction. Relating is the practical application of how to put this together in your work teams, your family life, and your organizational life. In the 21st century, in our hectic, fast-paced society, we've moved away from a capacity for stillness and resting in our own essence. There's a phrenetic quality in our lives with an over-emphasis on doing and accomplishing. MatrixWorks is a rebalancing of all three, whereby our value and worth aren't so dependent on what we do. We value doing, because human beings naturally want to create and accomplish, and we "want to put our labors where our love is." A healthy balance of all three creates a life that is more than just making a living.

Connection, Chaos, Consciousness
Spirals of Group Life

Maturity is the ability to find the similarities in the apparently different and the differences between the apparently similar. The goal is to differentiate and then integrate these differences.
- Ivonne Agarzarina

All relationships follow a simple but specific pattern. A healthy relationship will move through the entire cycle of this pattern, which corresponds to three stages: connection, chaos, and creative consciousness. If the pattern is stuck and the group does not navigate the chaos phase successfully, then it will act out or become stale, bringing out the worst in people, and the worst in the group. Usually the emergence of a scapegoat, a person in the group who represents that group's shadow side can mark this. Stuck in conflict and chaos, nothing grows, nothing new is created, and awareness is dim. But when we can navigate the sweet spot of chaos and conflict, the rewards are great. All parties will bring their best forward for the benefit of the whole. All parts will receive this benefit. All relationships represent the quality of flow.

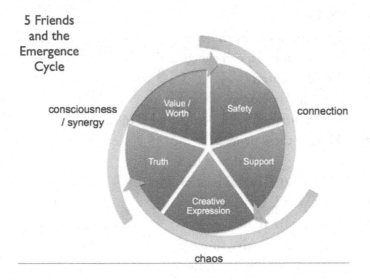

5 Friends
and the
Emergence
Cycle

consciousness / synergy

connection

chaos

THE THREE SPIRALING STAGES

These stages are not clear-cut and all the stages are present in any given interaction, it is just a matter of which stage will take precedence and move into the foreground. These stages are never complete, but rather continue to spiral into deeper levels of connection.

Inclusion / Connection:

Inclusion is about beginnings. Beginnings are magical times, rich with mystery and potency. Beginnings depend upon all parts being included. All parts need to know and be known, to see and be seen. At this stage, issues of safety, trust, belonging, support, connection, and contact are essential. The question at this stage is, "Am I in or am I out?"

To support this stage, warmth, love, attunement, and resonance are essential. When the field and the members begin to reciprocally inform each other, a state of balance occurs that resolves the paradox: "Can I be fully myself and also be a member of this group?"

Questions in the foreground of awareness during the Inclusion / Connection phase:

- Am I welcome?

- Am I safe?
- Can I speak my truth here?
- Where is my place in the group?
- How do I enter?
- What are the norms of the group?
- If I am different, will I be excluded or rejected?
- Who are these people?
- What are the subgroups here?
- What are the special relationships?
- What are the cliques?
- Who are my allies?
- Where can I receive support?
- Am I accepted, wanted, loved, cared about?

At this stage it is wise to track how included the members feel. It is important to make space to hear from each and every member and that each and every member feels valued and knows that their unique contribution matters. At this stage, the main job is to connect members to one another.

During the Inclusion / Connection phase the group facilitator has five tasks to attend to:

Task 1: Support the members to discover who is present. Members need to really hear, see, and feel each other. This is accomplished through interpersonal verbal & nonverbal interactions, and by naming subgroups and special relationships. These interactive encounters highlight our similarities, common themes, interests, and needs. Focusing on shared experiences supports a feeling of safety. This safety then forms the ground for accessing collective wisdom.

Task 2: Intentionally attune to the physical, emotional, psychological, intellectual, and physical needs of members.

Task 3: Clarify the container, the context, and the contract. Provide enough information for the participants to trust the container, boundaries, freedoms and contracts.

Task 4: Clarify the purpose and intention of the group and discover what has magnetized members to attend. This includes sharing the theoretical framework, values, assumptions, principles and practices.

Task 5: Name the themes of inclusion, including re-pattering in a template of belonging, safety, and moving 'in and out.'

The process of inclusion is never complete. When enough inclusion and safety has occurred, the group turns towards chaos and conflict.

Chaos / Conflict:

The main issue in conflict is power and dynamics of power. "Am I up or am I down?" At the grossest level, we often see conflict as opposing polarities. However, by shifting perception to where awareness is big enough to see the whole, the conflict dissolves. Conflict is re-framed as the doorway into creativity as it trains the capacity for the individual and group to notice, name and work with differences as gifts. Once an individual lets go of fear and avoidance of conflict they can live with more love and connection.

At the conflict stage the individual and the group explores:

Roles: The functions we assume in a group such as mother, teacher, helper, or organizer.

Stereotypes: Roles can become stereotypes. If and when this happens, the person becomes anonymous and we only see the role.

Archetypes: These are universal energy. At the conflict stage, archetypes arise and are played out through particular individuals. Without awareness, we act out roles that take on significance greater than the individuals' experience.

These can distort the group. By inviting and welcoming them in they become an opportunity for growth.

We have all experienced groups with a good deal of conflict and often we think that the groups we are a part of need conflict mediation. In actuality, many of these groups actually need inclusion. No one member, or the parties in conflict, actually feels valued and loved enough. Usually members have not discussed their fears about being rejected from the group if they disagree. If enough inclusion is cultivated, conflict will be much easier to weather, because members can trust that the group values them and that the group cares for them. When individuals feel loved and cared for, they are less fearful of differences.

The key to resolving conflict is to stay in relationship. Conflict is essential to move relationships past stuck places, and staying in relationship through conflict is essential in order to deepen. If individuals commit to the relationship conflict can be exhilarating, and liberating, and connective.

At the conflict stage, the main task is to normalize and bring forth basic differences. Make space for members to share the impact of other members, while holding the belief that conflict signals an attempt to move closer to one another.

Gifts of working with conflict: The four "F's"

- We claim Freedom to ourselves more fully.
- We experience Flexibility to shift from rigidity and fixedness to openness and possibility.
- We cultivate Fearlessness by staying with conflict until the higher order emerges.
- We embody Formlessness, allowing the energy of conflict to dissolve and reform in healthy ways.

Mutual and Transpersonal Connection: Creative Evolution

Through mutual connection there is a true resolution of the tension between belonging and autonomy. In Inclusion, we lay down the lines of connection. In Chaos and Conflict, we run energy through the lines of connection and welcome universal energies and archetypes. In Consciousness, the personal and particular unite with universal energies to express our human and divine nature. The group becomes the womb that grows the new individual. This new individual cares for the whole, as though it were the Self. It is where we respond to the basic question "have we been loved enough?"

As in the experience of the human condition, the life themes and stages show up in group development. Safety and support relate to the inclusion phase most clearly. Freedom and truth show up in chaos and conflict. Value and worth are part of Consciousness. In actuality, the themes are interdependent and are all present in some way at every group stage. Learning to track which ones are needs, which ones are resources in group members and the group as a whole is a useful skill for group facilitators.

The consciousness stage is where the fruit of healing arises for individuals and groups. This re-instills basic trust into the individual. They reconnect to the basic goodness alive within them and others. Individuals feel they can take new personal and emotional risks precisely because they are valued. Mutual connection is where the fruit of healing arises for individuals and groups.

During the consciousness stage of group life all that has not previously been loved or known love arises in its search for healing and it opens the door to the basic, universal longings we all share. Because these longings are universal, work that one member does is really work that all the members are doing, for they all share a piece of the longing that is arising in any given member. As deep risks are taken, the door to the transpersonal, to that which is indestructible in all of us, opens.

Widen Field of Awareness in Consciousness

- The four immeasurables are woven together with a personal field of warmth, attunement, resonance and love.
- One of our deepest wounds is explored: the betrayal of trust.
- The longing to be held in a field of love is experienced.
- The need for mutual connection is opened.
- Individually and collectively the five life themes are renegotiated: Safety, Support, Freedom, Truth, Value/Self Worth.

Relationships of any and every kind continuously cycle through these three stages. Pay attention to what relationships are in what stage, which ones are moving forward, and which ones may be stuck and need a nudge in the right direction. People need to have a positive experience in a group. When they can be held in enough safety that they can identify the traumatic experiences of past groups, healing can happen. The positive experience doesn't completely replace the healing, but it unhooks the past from creating the same circumstances (especially family of origin wounds) in the future. By becoming aware of the cycles of relationships while paying attention to the 4 pillars, we can facilitate greatness in ourselves, our relationships, and our group lives. In the next section, we will cover how to facilitate, plan, and design processes for group genius.

Practice with Reflection: Seeing systems

In this practice, we move from the direct perception of the physical towards seeing the energy and interconnectedness of the whole.

Step 1: Attention to the outer world. The physical body interacts with the world of form. Imagine yourself becoming a form through the production of cells in your body. Who are you becoming?

Step 2: Attention to the inner world. Who you are opens to and interacts with systems, and sparks fly. Imagine the part of you that's the source of abundant nourishment and deep connection. What magic do you possess with your very being?

Step 3: Attention to the secret world. Who you are and what you feel becomes aware of the invisible source beyond words, Bowing in service to the essential life force beyond and within us all. The secret is reflected in the breath, which takes it's root from the word aspire, which also means directing hopes and ambitions towards something. So the secret is the invisible direction a group or relationship wants to go towards, the essential life between two seemingly distinct entities. The secret is what connects the energy. The secret in a MatrixWorks context refers to the divine light we begin to see in one another. How much can you love? How much can love flow through every aspect of your daily life? In the face of challenge and decay, can you conjure the courage to stand and declare something else is possible?

Part Two
The Path: Facilitation

Facilitator Tools
Guidelines for Facilitation Mastery

A good leader is one, who by their presence, increases the
capacity for excellence in others, so that this excellence
continues in the presence or absence of the leader.
-Harvard Business Review

The path builds upon the ground of theory by incorporating practice. It is where we put our values and ideas into good use in groups. The optimum goal of the path is health, and we aim to accomplish this through skillful facilitation, which can happen from all members of the group. The word facilitate means "to make easy". Working with groups is assuming, contacting, and calling forth what is already there. Group facilitators are not creating connection and belonging, they are merely making it visible and more sustainable.

The group as a living system has within it a blue print of its own perfection. When this blue print is welcomed, it reveals a pattern of health and wholeness that could never have been created by the best group leader. The ultimate goal of the MatrixWorks class whatever the title or content is to give people direct access to their own wisdom. They say living systems have the answers inside: the acorn already has the full experience of the oak tree. The facilitator's aspiration is for people to strengthen a connection to that fundamental truth but experience it in relation to the larger group.

This section is a manual for people on how to facilitate living groups, how to get out of trouble, and how to intervene in a ways that stop destruction. The leader who can do this will provide a model of health by embodying the following capacities:

- Self organization: having a kind of agency to organize oneself and bring coherence out of chaos and into consciousness. Groups will learn to self organize and come up with better solutions than any facilitator could think of.
- Self regulation: anything living is constantly modulating itself. As a facilitator, you're playing the role of the neocortex or the attentive parent who says when it's time for a break or a walk. As a model for self-regulation, you help the group know when to apply the breaks and when to apply the accelerator.
- Self-correction: this is especially important for leaders. The most skillful and magical leaders can turn on a dime and they can change everything when they know the environment has changed and they need to change the way they're working with people.
- Self-transcend: letting go of an old identity in order to embody and express a new identity. Capacity for dissolution of the past so that something new can emerge. A part dies in order for something new to be born. When done right, people can get a new perspective on life.

Practice: These tips come from *Way of Council* practice, but can be applied appropriately to sharing as a facilitator. I share about myself to give you a sense of who I am, but also to develop safety and trust, as you would share openly and honestly about yourself when facilitating. Here are starting guidelines for sharing personally (and encouraging others to share vulnerably and fully):

- Speak from the heart. Speak your truth with kindness.

- Listen generously, from the heart
- Be lean of speech
- Be spontaneous
- Be 'for each other' and yourself: want the best for everyone
- Trust that all parts can fit together in a convergent whole: everyone who is here has a valued place

Reflection Question: How does this definition of leadership resonate with you? How does it relate to your own experience? What is your definition of leadership? What is your internal state when participating in groups? How do you facilitate when trying to bring safety and connection to a situation of confrontation and conflict?

Self-Regulation

The cave that you fear holds the treasure you are seeking.
- Rumi

Groups that rise are in a process of un-concealing themselves. Groups that fall keep hiding themselves. Alive groups engage in the continuous unfolding of each individual, of each relationship, and the group's purpose. Less inspiring groups only eat, work, and sleep, and then there's no orientation to creativity, possibility, or to serving.

When we are learning to facilitate in a living systems way (which means facilitating toward creating the conditions for emergent possibilities to happen) one of the necessary conditions is to be able to self-regulate. The first orientation to this way of working requires some courage to keep moving in the direction of what's not being expressed. This helps us move past the initial phases of group connection: Nice and polite, to tough and right, through the uncomfortable experience of differences towards more capacity for magic and flow. When the group is circulating energy, then the foot is off the break and we don't have to hold back our truths because we're in a free fall for what's possible and alive in the group. If we're going for this transformative group, then we're going to move through these cycles. As a facilitator, I won't be satisfied with the earlier stages, I'll want to nudge the group towards the magic.

I'm also using my own body as an instrument. If I start to feel bored or tired or disengaged, then I know that something is being left out of the group field, and I can ask the group to help bring it forward. For example, someone in the group may be holding back a piece without sharing. As a facilitator, I might recognize that I am feeling disengaged or bored, and that's my way of knowing that the information and energy in the group is not flowing in a continuous way. If I'm not feeling energized and alive, then I'm sensing a contraction there. I turn the group's attention towards it, while acknowledging that the contraction is okay and needed. The only way out is through.

As a facilitator, it's your job to first self-regulate to model the internal sense of presence for the group. Because of this, I refuse to intervene with someone if I don't feel clear with him or her. If I find myself annoyed or avoidant or full of a story, I'll wait until I find a heart connection that puts me into an essential relationship with that person. I won't confront until it's coming from a place of love and not power. When I find a space where Once I'm back to an open, accepting, and neutral place, I'll wait until we find each other to connect, and acknowledge the tension I noticed. For example, I might say: "it's painful to me when I feel like I can't make contact with you. I wonder if it's painful for you? And I wonder if contact is more available for us right now?" Connecting from an equal and loving field helps avoid power dynamics and the toxic pitfalls of facilitation.

These are potential traps and ways to cultivate self-regulation when you're off:

- **Monsters under the bed:** When I'm no longer in a state of vulnerability and neutrality, it's time to look at ways that fear, doubt, self-criticism, and counter-transference, can hook my mind and take me away from being in flow with the group. These hidden monsters interfere with my ability to perceive, rather than project. If I can't recognize and transform the negative emotions that arise, then they interfere with my ability to facilitate. It's a slippery slope when my anger gets unconsciously stirred in a group, or if I start to doubt the health or goodness of the group.

- **Projections:** Until we have done the right kind of inquiry and processing of our family of origin, we will overlay our personal family dynamics onto every group we enter. If you're really going to cultivate the conditions for a transformational group, then you have to go beyond the tip of the iceberg into your own family story, and skillfully learn how to recognize and process what's hidden beneath the surface. To see through that is a large part of clear perception of reality.

- **Meet unconscious resistance**: The fundamental element we are working with is the developmental edge. When we encounter the edge between seeing ourselves as a separate individual, and opening up to the truth that the whole group is also inside of us, we put up walls of resistance. As a facilitator, this is especially important to be aware of. You can work with this resistance by helping the group to see its wholeness. Pay attention to thematic language and listen for the common metaphors. Offering metaphors to the group assists in a group level intervention. For example, "it seems like this group really likes it when you get to do exercises in pairs. I wonder what that means for you? It's almost like you want to go on a date with just one person, like your needs won't be met in the group as a whole." Playing with the symbolism of behavior and reflecting that back to the group helps the group realize their inherent connection and come together: "I could be wrong here, but I notice that we jump into silence without letting it flow through, almost like we cut off the breath of exhalation." People will go deeper when the facilitator invites them into curiosity of behavior, rather than resistance.

When these monsters arise, it's imperative to know how to replenish yourself and how to recognize when you're not resourced:

- **Somatic Wisdom:** Energetically imagine a midline between the facilitators and each of the members of the group– look around at each person, saying to them in your own mind, that you're available, and you're welcoming them with a quality of presence and stillness that invites people to take their seat in the group. (See 4 pillars for full subtle energy practice).

- **Co-Facilitation:** Make contact with your Co-Facilitator if you have one. In MatrixWorks, we really believe in the advantage of co-facilitating – the two facilitators become as the banks of the river, creating safety so that the energy and dynamics of the group can flow more easily. If you are lucky enough to have a Co-Facilitator, make verbal contact with them in the group. You might say: 'I'm glad to sit across with you." You might also mention something about your relationship, and how you are excited to hold space with them in this group. Sharing like this makes the relationship between Co-Facilitators visible as a resource to the group– people will notice the ease and connection between you, and this will strengthen the feeling of safety in the group.

- **Supervision:** It's great if you can have a co-facilitator and there's trust and they can give you feedback, and even better if you can have some outside perspective on your blind spots. The work of healing (whether personally, in groups, or in business) is all about a commitment to ever-increasing awareness, and to know that it can never be complete, but can always be increasing.

- **Humility:** As a facilitator, it's not about you. You are simply providing the structure and the teachings for other people to contact the innate wisdom they already have, and then to back off and let others relate from that place. Your role as facilitator is to be aware if there are places in the matrix where the energy and the information can't flow, because someone needs attention to reintegrate with the group. There's a lot of gratitude and humility that comes with facilitation mastery, to become more awake and surrender; to be more receptive to the signs that come to point us in directions beyond ourselves.

To be successful in groups, we've got to be able to see from different perspectives. And that's what group work teaches us. There is a way in which seeing both sides of a polarity can be immobilizing. If one stays with it, without reactivity, something will emerge. Hakomi helps us study those things that we have organized out of our lives (because they may be coupled with pain), such as love, connection, and safety, and we want to include the things that we have excluded. Relationships and safety can help to organize back in and restore things in our unconscious that we have labeled as unsafe. Mostly, it's about taking in nourishment. Finding people whose hearts love you makes it easier to take in feedback and gives encouragement to go into the places that scare you. The phrase "redemption is in the margins" comes from Arnie Mendel in deep democracy work, and means that for whatever has not been included, there's a richness when we do finally include it. If you want the group to be alive and dynamic, then you'll always pay attention to what's present, what's missing, and what's in the margins.

Practice: "The Wheel of Awareness.[4]"

In the image below, The hub represents the experience of awareness itself -- knowing -- while the rim contains all the points of anything we can become aware of, that which is known to us. We can send a spoke out to the rim to focus our attention on one point or another on the rim. In this way, the wheel of awareness becomes a visual metaphor for the integration of consciousness as we differentiate rim-elements and hub-awareness from each other and link them with our focus of attention.

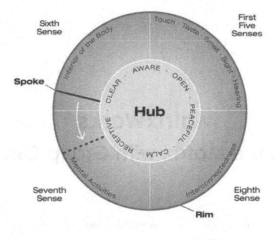

© 2007, 2014 Mind Your Brain, Inc.

Reflection question: What about yourself are you afraid to accept? What's hiding under the bed?

MatrixWorks
Weaving the Matrix with Group Geometry

*Currently one of the most accessible doorways to spiritually
is not individual meditation but small group work.*
-Otto Scharmer

G roups come together for a purpose. Declaring (or discovering) the
purpose up front serves as a guide for going forward with a unified
purpose. A part of the ground as it is worked with in MatrixWorks is
the belief that working with the power of the small group is really a
spiritual practice. Spiritual traditions have long known, and scientific
inquiry is now understanding, the principle of interconnectedness: that
the story of separation is a false story. Directly perceiving this truth of
interconnection is the spiritual fruit that can come from working with
groups.

In weaving the matrix, we develop a felt sense of how living systems
work, how each member is important, how diversity is important,
how synergy happens when you combine talents, and how the whole
is greater than the sum of its parts. This movement of energy and
information through all parts of the system is as vital to the aliveness
of group life as the movement of blood and nourishment and nutrition
to all parts of the human body.

Three Types of Group Organization:

Charismatic Leader, Talking Circle, Matrix

Working the geometry of a group is a powerful intervention. We name group design 'sacred geometry'. What this means is to design exercises and processes that allow each member of the group to be in face-to-face contact with every other member of the group in different configurations of twos, threes, fours, and small groups of eight to twelve. Each of these interactive exercises (that we will explore further in the Path section under 'exercises') establishes a line of connection between those participating, and ensures that the energy and information can move through all parts of the system. A vital principle of the power of working the geometry of the group and weaving the matrix is the deepening of safety that comes from interacting face to face.

Weaving the matrix is such a potent practice because we are making use of this fundamental group wisdom around differentiation and integration. In this process, group members are continuously coming together and coming apart. Repeatedly coming together and coming apart starts the process of being able to see ourselves in the other. It becomes safe to be ourselves, and safe to see others.

Intentional groups are a place where we can discover and work with the three poisons[5]: attachment, aversion, and ignorance. In every group, some people will annoy you, some people you'll fall in love with, and some you won't feel much of anything towards. The three poisons cause separateness and obstruct interconnection. Working with recognition of these feelings without being captured by them helps us to understand

and transcend suffering in groups. We need slight experiences with aversion, ignorance, and attachment because it's a part of our makeup. So if we can experience it with consciousness, then we can learn to see through it. In a group class, we can really increase our capacity to see ourselves as whole and as a part of the whole.

Co-facilitators help a group work through these challenges by representing a midline that balances a group. Most living things have a midline, a spine that connects the divergent parts to the center. Facilitators working together can provide the structure that makes it safe for the river of experience to flow. They provide a model of what health looks like by being open, vulnerable, and strong. Co-facilitators move the group towards creative evolution by modeling conflict and chaos in a healthy way. Relationships of any kind need feedback, safety, and respect.

The higher calling, or purpose, of the group is represented by the midline. Every group wants to go towards what is life affirming, what serves life. For many years in MatrixWorks I've been saying that the experience of this work is of being a part of a womb that grows the new individual who can care for the whole. Groups naturally crave an experience of wholeness, and facilitating interconnections guides the group in the way life organizes.

Practice: First establish the lines of connection between all members of the group. Then, as facilitators, look to see that the lines are kept open and communication can flow. When the group is a living system, we fall into a kind of magic of interconnection. Magic where we're not one, and we're not two. We are not each other, and we are not separate from each other. Make it possible for everybody to have contact with everybody else in the group.

Sub-Group Work: Divide the group into parts so they learn how to both honor the differences and integrate parts into the whole. This exercise helps the group to see what some people have in common, and what makes the group members different, while communicating that all parts and differences are welcome. These are a few examples of questions, but you can make up any questions to reflect your unique group. Standing in a circle, ask the members to step forward as you expose the existing connections among the participants:

- Who are the Yoga Students in the Room?
- Highlight the Men in the Room?
- Who are the Yoga Teachers?
- Who are the Parents? Grandparents? Who are the Dog Lovers? Cat Lovers?
- Who are the meditators?
- Who are the Therapist? Doctors, Lawyers?
- Who are the people in transition?

Working the geometry of the group in these different configurations allows for maximum connection between members and the creation of a very high feedback environment.

Tracking

An intervention refers to any comment, suggestion or recommendation that the consultant makes to the group in the service of accomplishing the task.
-W. Brendan Reddy, Intervention Skills

An intervention is a deliberate attempt to change or influence what is happening in the group. It can be an action or non-action which is verbal or non-verbal.
-David Patterson, GLT

When we are learning to facilitate in a living systems way, which means facilitating toward creating the conditions for emergent possibilities to happen, one of the most essential tools is to be able to track, or "to pay attention," to what's happening in oneself, between members of the group, and among the group itself. A facilitator is always paying attention to the group energy.

Health is the seamless flow of energy and information throughout a system, so living systems facilitation means paying attention to what parts of the system are resistant to the flow of energy and information. To cultivate the capacity to open to mystery, we learn to track what's going on inside ourselves, outside ourselves, and the space between: "I track myself and where is my attention drawn? Where do I stay a little bit longer?" Hone in on that and see what happens to me. Once the energy is identified, make contact and come into relationship with what you track.

After tracking, we then make contact with what we're noticing. Paying attention without taking action or making use of noticing is fruitless. Tracking and making contact is an ongoing process that's always happening in a group. It's a map for what will bring about the profound experience of safety in a group.

This methodology of tracking and contact comes from the Hakomi system, and through this process, people feel seen and have the experience of being heard. The fruit of safety is that we are able to communicate to the deeper parts of the members of the group. We learn that who they are and what they feel and think and say and do is welcome in the context of the group.

There's a willingness to go beyond the surface level (the 'nice and polite' realm of group life) when each member feels more held and safe by the group. Safety and support invite members to explore new territory and take risks. They can track the lines of inquiry into what might be possible, and what naturally wants to happen in the group. The process of paying attention and naming what is unseen enhances the intelligence of the relational field. For example: if I'm facilitating a group, I'm going to be paying attention to observable changes in expression and body language (someone might curl their toes, or have a smile, or turn away, or have a look of displeasure). I might then make contact to say "I notice you look perplexed" and see how the person responds (always tracking the body). When this happens repeatedly and group members begin to track and make contact, it creates a sense of being held in a safe container. The exquisite level of attention and noticing becomes a practice of mindfulness and meditation. When that is strengthened over time, people develop the courage to be vulnerable and they will risk showing parts of themselves that had previously been hidden, and also risk revealing secrets and shameful experiences that prevent members from fully participating in the present time group experience.

Remember that even if I notice something, and they respond "no[6]," even that response is good because it will take us in the direction we want to go (for example, I notice that someone feels sad and has a few tears coming on her cheek, and I say "I notice that something has touched you and I wonder if you feel sad." They may respond and say "I'm actually angry"). Don't be attached to your noticing; the goal is to follow their experience. Even if your contact statement is not agreed with, it will still keep the group moving towards what's possible, so you don't have to be afraid to make a mistake.

Something magical happens when we can really make contact with someone. Like we reach in with awareness and care and say something that touches the soul, and when we do that a joining takes place, and when it works it is a real diminishing of isolation and suffering that we all live in. Seeing through the mask and meeting from essential self to essential self. So much of modern day life lacks attunement, which is the missing experience we need. It's the same desire we have when we look down at our cell phones, creating an addiction to something we're not receiving. As we track and make contact, we build bridges of connection, strengthen them and break down walls to access greater depth of connection, which provides the safety to show up as our authentic selves, and puts us in touch with the connection that already exists.

Making Contact

Contact is letting the other know that we are paying attention and are able to register what is happening on and beneath the surface level. After we have 'tracked', we must make contact with what we have paid attention to and 'noticed deeply'. The purpose of Contact is to build safety, trust and a relational field that can deepen and provide a holding environment for the Group. A simple statement works to convey this attunement: if it seems a group member is impacted by something that has happened, I might say, "seems like that touches you, huh?" This allows the group member to recognize that their inner experience is being seen and is being welcomed into the group field. The key to this working is SIMPLICITY and enough openness in your wording that allows the other to confirm your contact or to correct it, if you have misperceived.

By this simple act of making contact, I am communicating to the Group Unconscious that I am awake, aware and willing to partner with the Healing Impulse that is present in the Group. This has a profound impact on the depth of healing that can happen in the group. Sometimes I believe that this is all that is needed to help a group unfold its potential: just awareness and attention to what is happening in the present moment! Soft, welcoming attention to what is presenting invites the next level of the mystery to 'un-conceal' itself, and, healing happens by itself, and we all are but the witness and recipients of this grace. Being led or following your impulse to lead groups in this way is compelling, terrifying, and one of the most nourishing experiences available to human beings.

Practice: Tracking the individual [7]

Simply put, Tracking is Paying Attention to verbal and non-verbal aspects of communication.

In the group, we hold the intention to be receptive and responsive to what each person is experiencing in the moment. This requires a capacity to let information come to you rather than going out to get it. At first, we may only have hunches, guesses about what is happening inside another. However, with practice, we start to perceive more directly and learn how to check this out with the other. The information we receive is often telling us in large or small ways that the individual(s) feel seen, heard, received, safe or not; and how this matches or challenges their internal beliefs about themselves, other people, groups and the world. It is as if the 'mind of the body' speaks a special language we can learn if we attend to the non-verbal aspects of communication. Notice what you can notice about the following:

Tracking body: How is the body held: stiffly, loosely, openly? Does it reflect Earth, or Water or Air or Fire? How does it relate to gravity, to space? Does it seem to draw you in or hold you out? What is the energy field around the body? Is it animated or subdued? Do the eyes shine or do they hide? Does the smile warm your heart? Does the smile seem to mask a pain? If this body could speak, what do you imagine it would say? What is the overall level of Tension/Relaxation?

Posture: Is the posture relaxed or rigid; comfortable and flowing or held and protective? If the Posture were expressing a need, what do you imagine the need would be: for contact? For space? For attention? For appreciation? Do any particular hand or face gestures seem to fit with the posture, or, feel incongruent with the posture?

Pace: How fast or slowly do the individuals in the group speak, think, move or interact? Do some have their 'foot on the brake' while others are pressing the accelerator? How patient are the Speedies with those more Slow? How pushed do the Slow ones feel by the speed of faster pace participants?

Feelings and Needs: How freely are feelings and needs expressed? Which ones seem hard to acknowledge? What do you sense are hidden 'longings' in the group members? Who seems to need attention from whom? Where are the natural affinities and allies in the group? Who seems cautious of/ afraid of whom? Is there a sense that nourishment is available for everyone in the Group?

Energy: What is the level of aliveness in participants? Do some seem over-stimulated? Under-stimulated? Is there a quality of play, humor, and delight? Or, is the energetic quality more serious, measured and careful? What metaphor arises for you as you experience the energy of this group? What calls your attention by its lack of presence in the group?

Health and Hidden Potential: What is the great health of each member of the Group? The Group as a Whole? What is their 'hidden potential'? What is just beneath the surface, waiting for an invitation to emerge as a glorious gift? What is the experience that wants to happen in this moment? How do we, as facilitators, support the Relational Intelligence of this particular group to 'make magic' through human connection that calls forth the hidden potential?

Practice: Tracking Relationships

Who sits by whom?
Who talks after whom?
Who talks a lot?
Who talks a little?
Who talks through using non-verbal language?
Who is paired with whom?
Who are the members of the natural Triads?
Who leads with feelings?
Who needs food for the left brain to feel safe?
Who needs to be invited "in"?
Who is sensitive to power dynamics?
Who is the oldest/youngest?
Who has the most/least confidence?
Who are you drawn to?
Who are you not drawn to?
Who do you ignore?
Who do you imagine is drawn/not drawn/ignores you?
Who do you see as a "natural leader"? Why?
Who do you trust?
Who do you envy?
Who do you feel more skilled than?
Who has access to their deep inner experience?

Who comes alive in connection?
Who orients to invisible dynamics in the Field?
Who focuses on Task?
Who focuses on Relationship and Nourishment?
Who is longing to be met with strength?
Who is defended against Intimacy?
Who is your peer?
Who understands that you are human?
Who touches your soul?
Who has a 'hungry spirit to do good?

Practice: Tracking the geometry.

The following are ways for the group members to track how well the group is woven together, and learn to make healing interventions as a team. Tracking the energy at the level of the group moves the focus of attention from oneself to others in the group. It makes each member an individual *and* the group, to broaden awareness of the whole.

Flying fish: a moment of magic when the group gels

Spark: delicious energy that could go into conflict or could fall in love

Swirl: not getting to the point, disorganization, not landing on the truth

Internal squeeze: Someone in the group uncomfortable, holding back

5 friends: where along this spectrum is the group? What does the group need to reach the next level?

Hot spots: tender, vulnerable topics that trigger members of the group

Near and far: who is resonating with the topic, who is neutral?

In and out: paying attention to who is included, and who is left out

Practice: Tracking the connection spiral of groups

In Pairs or Triads, explore this primary pattern of relationships
"Nice and Polite"
"Tough and Right"
"Inquiring and Reflecting"
"Magic and Flow"

Reflection questions: What do you observe in someone's behavior? In your own behavior? How might you become curious in a way to make safe contact?

Planning: Context, Container, and Content
Planning a Course of Facilitation

G iven all of these theoretical frameworks and tools, we can move into action. Setting out to work on any transformational process requires foresight, planning, and preparation. To begin your work of bringing MatrixWorks principles and practices, we recommend designing a plan within these elements: context, container, and content. These guidelines will help you adapt our theory to your unique situation and leadership style.

Context

This word comes from the Latin 'contextus', which means a joining together, scheme, or structure. This is particularly relevant in our MatrixWorks context because MatrixWorks means to join by weaving, and that is the ultimate goal and outcome of our work. As you begin to plan and design a process for MatrixWorks, you will first define the context you are working within. Knowing the strengths, weaknesses, and goals of your current work or life relationship is essential to creating the ground from which to grow. As with coaching, we have to understand our present situation along with a future goal if we are to have any hope of realistically achieving that desired outcome.

The context for a group comes alive through activating the four competencies of leadership: Design, presentation, co-facilitation, and collective intelligence. Design relates to the balanced planning of activities, exercises, and themes relevant to group evolution. Presentation is the competence to share ideas and information clearly. Co-facilitation represents a midline intention for the group to organize around, and it serves as the model for collaboration and working through differences. Collective intelligence is the sum of all the genius in the room, and it is accessed when all the parts are able to offer their gifts in dynamic relationship.

Competencies in these four areas provide the structure for creative group emergence to flow. The following chapter explores context in further depth.

Container

The container defines how you set up a space for change to happen. You may be familiar with the term "creating space," which relates to the concept of a container. Not just any space will do. For example, your office or home may already have spaces that trigger the same habits and routines. Stepping outside of that space creates the possibility for something new to happen. That's what we mean by container. Creating the conditions that are safe enough for people to explore new and healthy ways of relating.

Any member of the group can participate in creating the container for a group. The necessary conditions for an evolutionary container relate to what neuroscientist and psychologist Rick Hanson, Ph.D. describes as the three fundamental needs for humans: safety, satisfaction, and connection. Safety drives us to avoid harm. Satisfaction leads us to approach rewards. Connection encourages us to attach to others. When a facilitator can successfully work with the group to fulfill these needs, the group releases limits to flow and creativity. The following chapters detail ways to cultivate the container.

Content

It seems accurate that the word for information and experiences is the same as the word that means satisfied, peaceful happiness. Choosing which pieces of learning to include will be defined by the context, but they will also be defined by that which will satisfy and nurture. Design just enough to get it moving, then let emergence happen in relationship with feedback from the group. (Like parenting, the group is its own being).

Content should be balanced between presenting neuroscience, geometry, and mindfulness. When mind, body, and spirit are in harmony, we reach contentment. These three diverse elements of content correspond to the mind, body, and spirit of groups. The following chapters will detail the content we explore in MatrixWorks classes and consulting.

Genius Groups do three things all the time, simultaneously. These are:

1) Attend to relationship (how is the energy/information flowing between people in the group?)
2) Accomplish task (as facilitators, make sure you're clear about the task, so maybe one of your first intentions will be to clarify the task of the group)
3. Create/cultivate/sustain cultures that are nourishing, support wellbeing, and the ability to manifest care, creativity, and compassion.

These three capacities form three points of a triangle and area always happening in high functioning groups. As a Facilitator/Co-Facilitator you pay close attention to how these three capacities are present or how they are missing.

Context

If you don't set an intention first thing in the day,
you'll be following somebody else's by noon
- Source unknown

The context relates to the background or climate of your present situation. It is like gathering research and data on the way things are, and comparing them to the way things could be. By setting a context, you not only stay grounded for yourself, but you also provide a ground for the relationship. We can't really know where we are going if we don't know where we are.

The context also contains the purpose of coming together. We need a compass to guide our work so we can stay on course. Intentions can be a powerful way of containing the direction of energy and growth that gets created in a change initiative. The compass that we orient towards is increased awareness of the whole, and I don't think anything increases awareness like intentional group work. A journey through group work is nothing more than expansion of awareness through a real-life meditation in relationships. So the Compass really is awareness; that's the direction we're going in. In Jung's work the mandala is a symbol for wholeness, a unique way the parts and the whole fit together, and represents the integrated self. The evolution that happens when people have an experience with MatrixWorks is they leave feeling more whole, and that their life is a mandala.

Setting the context sometimes brings up the question of whom to invite to a group. From my experience, I more and more trust that the people who *show up* to the group *are* the right people. It really is the healing impulse that wants to happen. We gather a group with intention and the healing impulse can express itself. We can set the initial intention, and then the healing impulse will take it from there. We can learn about the big archetypes guiding the group by asking participants to reflect on the questions: "why have I come? What drew me to the class? What is my purpose in being here?" Then, we simply listen to the answer that arises, trying to provide the experiences that we need in order to live a meaningful life in the 21st century, both as an individual and in right relationship with all that is.

Practice: To connect to your purpose

In your journal, reflect on each of the following questions. Which of these keys is your:

Gift
Challenge
Wound
Missing in your life
Need more of in your relationship

Enlightened Feminine Leadership

One example of context is a class we teach called Enlightened Feminine Leadership. This class (and MatrixWorks in general) tends to attract more women than men, which sets up a different context or tone for the group development. Because women (and balanced men) tend to have a natural understanding of this work, we can weave together and give voice to some big themes that women naturally intuit. It seems important to give Feminine Leadership its own section because it is a large part of our focused work.

The context of Enlightened Feminine Leadership supports and uplifts the inherent gifts women possess by weaving together archetypal themes: Enlightenment, intuition, sacred feminine, leadership, embodiment, healing. It welcomes women to rebalance leadership from the old story of separation and domination to the new story of possibilities of love and connection. Creating the context helps ground big ideas into present awareness, insight, and action. We begin to envision together what a new model of Leadership might entail. The following practice is a staple in our Enlightened Feminine Leadership offering.

Practice: Communicating with Mitochondria

We take responsibility for the context of our lives and work by becoming more aware. To increase awareness, we have to continually resource ourselves. The deepest resource we can access is the wisdom in our own bodies. One way to do this is by getting in touch with our mitochondria, which exist in every cell of the body. Mitochondria make up ten percent of our body weight and produce the energy of life we need to live.

Wisdom Traditions and science alike say we inherit our mitochondrial energy from our 'Mother Lineage' and pass it on to our offspring. Therefore, our maternal wisdom lives in our physical body as the mitochondria. Through this embodied lineage, we can imagine communication with our mother lineage to heal mother wounds and access the wisdom that accumulated through time to reach us today.

A lack of oxygen signals to cells that it's time to die, and lack of oxygen make the mitochondria less efficient at turning glucose into the energy cells need to function. If there is a lack of energy, vitality, or life force in our being, we can use our attention to connect with the original intention of the mitochondria to support life. In the burnout of modern times, we can restore our own connection to the blueprint of perfection inside our cells.

Begin to dialogue with your mitochondria by setting up an "Empty Chair" exercise. Inquire about how they are and if they have a message for you.

- Work in groups of two or three, taking on the roles of Experiencer, Guide and Supporter. The Experiencer sits or stands with the Supporter behind and the Guide in front. The Guide invites the Experiencer to focus on her Mitochondria, conducting a body scan that moves from her feet up to her head and back down again. Allow several minutes for this to deepen.
- The Guide asks the Experiencer: "if your Mitochondria could speak to you, what would they say?" Repeat 10-15 times, allowing for new messages from the mitochondria to arise with each new question round.
- The Supporter writes down what the Experiencer says and reads the notes back to the Experiencer at end of the session, asking the Experiencer to reflect on the process.
- Shift roles: Each person has a turn at all three roles. End with the whole group sharing about the impact of the experience. Ask the group to reflect on the opportunities and challenges of expressing Enlightened Feminine Leadership in their lives.

Container

*A social environment can change the relationship between
a specific gene and the behavior associated with that gene.
Changes in social environment can thus change the transcription
of our genetic material at the most basic cellular level.*
- The Commission on Children at Risk, Hardwired to Connect

Initial conditions set the tone for all living systems. Whatever conditions are present in and around anything living (e.g. A person, plant, group, organization) at the beginning determine the tone of the life of the entity. Not that you can't change and transform the qualities, but there is a tone that ripples through. Consider some beginnings that happened in your life. In what capacity did they set the tone for the continuation of the experience? When the initial conditions are toxic, the group is likely to suffer from some aspects of toxicity. When the initial conditions are health, the group has potential to grow into a healthy group.

Setting a container as a fundamental ground is about designing the right balance of what Rick Hanson calls the three fundamental needs: attention to need for safety, need for satisfaction or nourishment, and need for connection. Attending to those needs of safety, satisfaction, and connection, allows participants to fully enter into the present moment, which is where healing happens. When those experiences are actual or cultivated the brain doesn't know the difference and we build the resource we need to live a life of choice and to be responsive.

The goal is to give an early experience of something new happening. The brain hungers for the rush of dopamine pleasure transmitter that comes from novelty. When novelty is activated in the reward circuit in the body, we learn more easily by forming new neural networks. The role of ritual and ceremony ties into the need for novelty: rituals allow us to bring together a sense of familiarity along with novelty for something new. Through use of body expression, silence, and creating an interpersonal matrix, the deeper part of each individual says, "aha! Something new may happen here!" Then the container becomes the safe womb that gives birth to the new individual.

The responsibility of a MatrixWorks facilitator is to create an environment of goodness that reflects the goodness we know is possible inside people. Our intention is to give people an experience that they're longing for, that they may not even know is the missing experience. The outer environment needs to reflect and be attuned to and respond to the needs of the group. We assume that people have come because of an inner knowing that more is possible in themselves and in relationships. The healing impulse has brought them to a context to meet a need of which they may not even be conscious.

The reason that the container is so important is analogous to human biology: you can remove the nucleus of a cell and the cell will still live, but you can't take away the protective membrane. The container is like the membrane that denotes protection and safety. The membrane is semi-permeable so it can receive information, and certain things (that may be habitual or less life-affirming) can stay out. We can choose to work with those less than skillful things, but we don't allow them to contaminate our group container. We're not rejecting competition or aggression, but rather we want to work with them so the true nature of alignment or human capacity can come forward. We want to shift dis-regulation[8] into something with more possibilities so that there's less acting out in groups. The container principle draws from what we understand about secure attachment and the necessity for nurturing relationships, whether we are children or adults. An authentic part of the self won't come out to play unless there is safety among relationships.

As women, we intuitively understand this. Part of the purpose of this course is to give women the opportunity to claim what they already know about the power of safety and satisfaction and connection, and use it for our interactions in the world. Our leadership creates environments that are safe, and it really brings out the best in others.

Here are some practices for cultivating the container:

- Silence: Meditation allows us to notice the resistance to entering the realm of silence, so we can let go of what we know so something else can emerge. The capacity of leadership and facilitation to tolerate silence opens the doorway for other members to be silent. Through silence, group members can identify the moments of spark when the group comes together and the whole becomes bigger than the sum of its parts. Silence allows us to drop into presence, creative flow, and emergence. Silence and sound are the most important factors that move a group from being regressive to transformational. Like the body that needs rest to recover, the healing impulse happens if you just pause.

- Rituals: The main function of a ritual is the intention to create sacred space and time. Sacred can mean focused (not necessarily religious), it is a way to make a boundary by setting a container for the time. The facilitator has rituals that he or she does, and the group needs to somehow signal to the members of the group that what is about to happen is different than what has happened before. Rituals help us make use of energy and structure for the beginning, middle, and end of a session. Rituals in the beginning build safety. Middle rituals involve time structures and how we start and end each day (for example: a moment of mindfulness, breaks, 20 minutes of stretching after lunch, closing the day with gratitude). End rituals signify a threshold between what people have experienced in the class and returning to their lives to integrate the learning (these include graduation, gifts, and information to support their continued learning and stay in relationship). The most important thing about the rituals is they are intended to get at the unconscious meta-level essence of the class. If it is done without too much of a heavy hand, it seeps in, massages the unconscious, and makes more possible.

- Preparation: Before the class starts, orienting to the needs of the participants can help you prepare for what each particular group may need. I try to find out what calls them to come to a class. We send an orientation letter with logistics and questions to prime the pump and also a practice for people to do before they come to class. We make a welcome bag that has a mystery message (the message is framed as a message from their higher self). When people arrive we ask them to describe themselves in their name tag with some questions. For example: name 3 things that you love a lot, or one thing you love and one that scares you.

- Providing nourishment: Giving the best nourishment by feeding people well gives people a sense they are treating themselves. It communicates that they are held in a place of high esteem or value, which results in people feeling seen, and appreciated, and honored. We don't see things as they are, but as we are. Imagine what becomes possible when people are seen as their best (value, beauty, attention) from the start.

- Gifts: Giving a small gift of matrix or crystal bead, my intention is that it becomes a transitional object that they take with them but it is a symbolic representation of carrying the experience they've had.

- Time Structure: Time boundaries help the structure flow, while signaling that you value everyone's time. Every group has a beginning, middle, and end. As facilitators, we take responsibility for keeping track of time and tending to these phases.

The beginning phase is really about establishing safety and connection because the more safety, the deeper and more productive the group can be.

The middle phase could be spent really working issues with people, or divide into little work teams to solve a problem. It's the working phase, whether that's inter/intra personally, a time that is lively. Working through tasks and chaos needs to be approached with the potential of simultaneously being nourishing to the members. If energy is lagging or a group is stuck, the facilitator may need to do something to encourage movement of energy. In MatrixWorks, we are always looking for the coherence and energy level of the group at any stage of the group's life. We support the feelings, aliveness and dynamic interactions as the group develops. Facilitators continue to check in with their own body/mind intelligence to get clues about the unfolding of the group's capacity.

The ending phase is about stitching together the territory that's been covered. This phase recaps the themes, issues, resolutions, open wounds, unexplored territory, and group accomplishments. It encourages the group to feel a sense of completion as the group (or group cycle) comes to an end. There's a great hunger in humans for sense of completion. Facilitators need to know and remember that it is common for a group to not want to stop when it gets going. Facilitators have to put the brakes on and prevent peoples' enthusiasm from being excessive. Once there's been a peak experience in a group, then the group needs a break to rest. Let them have that sense of completion and accomplishment. If you try to rush into the next issue or try to duplicate what's just happened, you lose the sense of rhythm you have with the group. As facilitator be mindful of what is reasonable for the time, energy, structure, and contract that you have with the group.

Practice: Pebble in pond

"Your truth is needed here. Your truth is welcome here"

Hakomi uses this technique to introduce people to a shift in consciousness to move people into a deeper level. It is a simple way to make use of the power of mindfulness [9] by letting go of anything you were concerned about and coming into the present moment. When we have these unconscious beliefs, we seek out the experiences that confirm our bias. But if we work with it, we update our files to have a new core belief that attracts healing and aliveness. Contacting core beliefs through this process offers the option to transform the beliefs.

<u>Here is an example of this approach</u>: Invite the group to become mindful and relax into themselves. Then share with them: *"I'm going to offer a potentially nourishing phrase. You don't have to believe this statement, it's more like a pebble in a pond, and you can just notice what happens all by itself when you hear me say* **"you are lovable"**[10]. (Say this three times and give a few minutes for people to register what has happened for them). *And you can become aware of any thoughts or feelings that come up. Just pay attention to what your inner awareness wants to communicate to you."*

Encourage them to think about how they responded– was it a shift in their sensations, maybe a feeling arose, maybe there was a thought, whatever happened, it is OK. Then invite sharing (popcorn style, or go around the circle). Through this sharing, we can see some of the things we need to attend to in this particular group.

If someone has a core belief that the statement isn't true, then they will have some reaction to it. The first time I heard this it was framed as: *"Your life belongs to you,"* and I was overworked and my reaction was *"like hell it is!"* The purpose is to bring forth an unconscious belief to the surface. Awareness of these unconscious beliefs helps people to deepen in the transformation process.

Practice: Warming up the room.

Turn to a person next to you and ask open-ended questions:

"What brought you here tonight? What's something you want to learn that will help you live your life? What risks are you willing to take?"

Open-ended questions help people feel safer, and build the lines of connection for a new group, or deepen the connections for existing relationships. If members talk to each other first, then they feel more relaxed and open to new possibilities. All it takes is making connection with one person, and the social engagement system is activated. This exercise can be done on it's own or after beaming a welcoming.

Reflection Question: Again and again we find these values emerge in healthy groups. On a scale of 1-10, how would you rate your groups along these healthy values?

1. Free expression of group and individual gifts
2. Love as an experience through connection and relationship
3. Mutuality and autonomy
4. Chaos/conflict as a necessary part of creativity
5. Feedback/information as avenues for a system to see itself and evolve
6. The ability to live with the inherent paradoxes of groups and life
7. Present moment awareness
8. Shared leadership
9. The ability to meet the needs of the members
10. The ability of the group to accomplish its task

Content
How this class is organized

I've learned that people will forget what you said, people will forget what you did, but people will never forget how you made them feel.
- Maya Angelou

In a MatrixWorks class, we present a balance of theory, experiential exercises, and reflections for practical application. In our first class, we will focus primarily on experience and application. We begin any MatrixWorks offering with connection to lay the ground for evolutionary group genius. We're trying to help people get in touch with, or remember, the depth of their longing for connection. Rick Hanson uses the phrase "connection is our biological imperative." It is the way we are organized as living systems. Living systems have a biological imperative for connection.

The content, whatever it is, is presented in an experiential learning modality, because experience changes the brain. The design is to move on a continuum from *information* to *transformation*. Our bias is that people remember experiences. The design really focuses on what is the right relationship between experience and theoretical understanding. Making meaning from experience and information changes the brain, creating new neural networks that allow us to experience a new reality.

No matter what the theme of the class, the content is drawing on cutting edge and current information from the study of the body, study of how the brain is organized, mindfulness, and empathetic relationships. This is true whether it's a class for couples, for women, for leadership, groups, and conflict.

Designing a class requires a balance of theory and experiential activities with the purpose of moving towards greater connection and wholeness. Every MatrixWorks class has elements of how to approach and experience empathetic relationships. People in MatrixWorks classes have an experience of feeling they are held in hearts and minds of others who have a self. That's how we build a self. The following are ways to orient towards healing and emergence when designing class content:

- Mindfulness: Every class focuses on the power of mindfulness, and the direction toward really understanding the power of awareness. Becoming aware of yourself and your impact on others and the field.

- Neuroscience: understanding of brain and body connection.

- Emotional Intelligence/Geometry: Understanding the architecture of group life, what makes groups come alive, what makes groups go numb, and how to facilitate dynamic creativity through healthy relationships.

- Creation of a high feedback environment: where the participant's core beliefs, internal assumptions and mental models about themselves, others and the world can be explored, corrected and brought into alignment with the present time and current choice.

- Creation of multiple group structures and processes: The group members participate in Task Groups, Whole Group Processes, Small Fish Bowls, Small Group Dialogue, Skill Building Groups, etc. Through participation in these multiple contexts, participants begin to expand and re-pattern their capacity to connect, to join with others in ways that are nourishing, warm, resonant, attuned, loving and they also become more effective in accomplishing tasks. They develop the skills found in healthy, high-functioning groups: attend to relationship; accomplish tasks; nourish members.

- Design always follows the pattern of connection, chaos, and consciousness. In connection, the focus is on weaving the matrix with group geometry by facilitating connections with self, other, and the group. Once safety is established by connection, we move to chaos by exploring differences (while maintaining connection). The dynamic experience of feeling connection and difference without polarizing will naturally move a group into evolutionary creativity, the final stage of group consciousness.

Class Themes

There are many themes that draw groups to learn together. Here are some examples of the classes MatrixWorks offers to different groups:

Enlightened Feminine Leadership: This course provides a new model of leadership for women and men grounded in the 'connective edge'... a feminine quality that men and women can develop, and that many women seem to naturally possess. These unique times require a more radical inclusion of all voices and all needs: women leaders have cultivated this skill. Women leaders know how to engage others in dialogue and conversations that lead to deeper and more collaborative solutions to complex problems. This course rests on the foundation of the interconnectedness of all life and the calling that all women have to express a deep care and commitment to serve Life. We need other humans from cradle to grave, and women can learn and teach a model of Leadership that expresses the power and truth of interdependency.

Evolutionary Leadership: This class aims to address leadership challenges in the spheres of education, healthcare, business and therapy. Seasoned practitioners who hold leadership positions in each of these four spheres come together in this class to learn and learn to teach radical collaboration. Mindfulness as a leadership skill is key to twenty-first century leadership and functions as an anchor in this training. In depth experience of the power of embodiment and the cultivation of somatic intelligence makes this course an extraordinary opportunity for cutting edge facilitation competency. If you want to help your organization thrive in a time of chaos, this is the class for you.

Group Genius Accelerator: The MatrixWorks model of Connection, Chaos and Consciousness provides the foundational ground for creating Group Genius. In this revolutionary process you will gain the skills and experience to unleash the Genius in your future teams or groups. This work has been successfully implemented to corporate, non-profit, and community groups.

Patterns of Relationship: For couples, mother-daughter, father-son, siblings, and all family relationships, including family owned business relationships. Explore the Living Systems principles of MatrixWorks as they apply to your close relationships. Discover together new levels of creativity, collaboration and connection.

Surfing the Edge of Chaos: Chaos is a part of the natural cycle of any complex living system that occurs before a reorganization at a higher level of order and complexity. According to complexity theory: anything living alternates between order and chaos, being and becoming. This class is about exploring the 'sweet spot' of chaos and conflict as doorways to greater creativity and deeper connection.

Mother/Daughter Bond: Offering a unique model of leadership, based on the powerful Feminine principle of 'connecting the disconnected'- sometimes referred to as the Connective Edge in women's leadership, we intend to engage a radical inclusion of the Mother-Daughter archetype in our program. We will explore the gifts, the shadows, the potentials and pitfalls, the betrayals and reconciliations. We will call forth the fundamental principle of the Interconnectedness of all life, and have a direct experience of the yearning we feel in our being to express deep care for all Life. We will gain clarity about how we can serve life in our work and in our relationships. We will learn how to "mother" and "daughter" the world. Experiencing the power and truth of our interdependency in this class will become our inspiration for creating a world that knows the true value of being human in relationship. We will go far together.

Community Approach to Couples: We invite Couples who want to enliven their relationships to participate in a unique approach to understanding your Couple Dynamics within the larger context of Group and Community. Using both MatrixWorks and Hakomi methods to cultivate and strengthen the Resources available to Couples, this dynamic class will renew, restore and revitalize your ability to create Sanctuary for each other and your family.

Class Timelines
A Typical Workshop Schedule

The following is an example of a typical schedule we may plan for a MatrixWorks Workshop. It is by no means the only way, but an example of how we structure our time for our participants.

Day 1 (5-8PM)

5:00 - 5:30 PM Images, Mingling, Partner Exercises
5:30 - 6:00 PM Sub-Groups
6:00 - 6:15 PM BREAK
6:15 - 7:00 PM Choosing Pods/Groups
7:00 - 7:30 PM Special Partner Exercise in Pods
7:30 - 8:15 PM Whole Group, Overview of Schedule, Completion

Day 2 (9:30 AM to 6:30 PM)

9:30 - 10:00 am Opening-Whole Group Process Pod 1
10:00 - 11:30 am BREAK
11:30 - 11:45 am Process Pod 2
11:45 am - 1:15 pm LUNCH with Pod
1:15 - 1:45 pm Process Pod 3
1:50 - 3:20 pm Play Break
3:20 - 3:35 pm Process Pod 4
3:40 - 5:10 pm Process All Groups Simultaneously
5:15 - 6:00 pm Collect Learnings
6:00 - 6:30 pm Closure

Day 3 (8:30 AM to 2:00 PM)

8:30 - 9:00 am Opening Whole Group

9:00 - 10:30 am Process

10:30 - 10:45 am BREAK

10:45 am - 12:15 pm Process

12:15 - 12:45 pm LUNCH with Pod

12:45 - 1:30 pm Process

1:30 - 2:00 pm Whole Group Completion

Exercises
3 spirals and Practices

Exercises to Help De-Mystify and Unlock the Magic of Facilitation

Now that we've explored all of the foundations for design and planning, we offer teachings and exercises to explore in facilitating aliveness in groups. The main objective as a facilitator is to be able to recognize and guide groups through the three spirals of connection and inclusion, conflict and chaos, and creative emergence and consciousness. The goal is to facilitate health.

Radical Inclusion

In the beginning of a group, or during any new phase in group life, all parts need to know and be known, and need to see and be seen. As the principles and practices of inclusion unfold, members begin to understand the unique and necessary role they play for the whole. The hidden potential of the group to know itself as whole living system becomes manifest. The unification of opposites (like the archetypal sperm and egg) in group life begins to invoke more life for individuals and the community.

The energetic field that must be created to fully support the potential of this gesture is one of warmth, love, attunement, and resonance. When the field and the movement pattern begin to reciprocally inform each other, a state of balance occurs that resolves the paradox of the question: "Can I be fully myself and also be a member of the group?"

The facilitator's role at the inclusion phase is similar of that of the "good enough mother" (Winnicott) who will support members to connect with each other through the building of interpersonal connection.

The process of inclusion is never complete in a group. It is always happening and always needed. When enough inclusion and safety has occurred in a group, the group's attention will turn more toward the stage of chaos and conflict and working with differences. When the differences are worked in a satisfactory way, the group moves naturally toward mutual connection. It is at the stage of Mutual Connection that there is a true resolution of the tension between belonging and separating, between being a member and being autonomous. It is at this stage of mutual connection that the group has become the womb that grows the new individual. And, the new individual cares for the whole of the Group as though it were Self.

The facilitator's role is to help the group discover the inherent unity that allows all the parts of the system to work together to create emergent genius. In the inclusion and connection phase, the following questions can help guide the facilitator:

- Who is here?
- What are the pre-existing networks of connection? How can I help this group see itself?
- How do I attune to the needs of individuals, interpersonal connections, and the whole?
- What is the purpose and intention of this group and what Might it become?
- How do I recognize when someone is feeling included or not? Who needs to be brought into the group, and by whom?
- How can I make space for the quieter voices to be included?
- Can I remember to trust that whoever is most 'out', holds the gift that the group most needs?

- Can I name the basic principles of the group as they arise, in a way that contacts and validates the present moment experience of the members?
- In a simple and profound way, facilitating Groups as Living Systems is about assuming, contacting, and calling forth what's already there.
- We assume that as a Living System, the Group has within it a blue print of its own perfection. This blue print, when welcomed to come forth, reveals a pattern of health and wholeness that could never have been imagined by the best facilitator.

The facilitator assumes that the members of the group already belong. He or she supports the recognition of this belonging by assuming that they will provide each other with keys of information. These keys, when attended to, can unlock hidden treasures of information that allow the members to enter the group and recognize their belonging. We are not creating connection or belonging, we are simply making it visible.

To align with this "Inherent Treatment Plan" of the living system of the group is one of the most satisfying and nourishing experiences of working in this way. It is as if we are allowed to place our finger on the creative pulse of the universe and, in so doing, are enlivened by the mystery herself. The perception of Wholeness emerging from the parts of the system is a direct experience and we know we belong to the universe and each other.

The entire process of MatrixWorks is about training awareness, ever broadening awareness, ever deepening awareness, and ever clarifying awareness. This is why we call the first phase, "Radical Inclusion."

Practice: Tracking the cycle of group life.

Apply the 3 spirals of connection/inclusion, chaos/conflict, and creative evolution/emergence to two or three of your groups. Find one group that has gone through all 3 stages, another that got stuck on chaos, and another that is still in connection. Use the cycle of awareness to identify an intervention that would help move the group to the next phase. How did applying that equation facilitate the group to become a living system or not? What are the qualities of groups at each of 3 stages? Is there a stage you prefer?

Reflection Questions: Observer Tasks for Connection Phase

Draw up a seating chart and diagram the interactions of "The Interpersonal Matrix"
Who is talking to whom?
Who is not talking?
Who is including whom, and how?
Who's initiating?
Who's responding?
Who isn't joining?
Observe where people are sitting and the impact on relationships and interactions. In order to identify patterns of interactions, list the order in which each person talks. What meaning do you make of these patterns? Bring these observations into the awareness of the group, and watch how awareness shifts behavior.

Chaos
The Expression of Conflict, Control, and Confrontation

The main issue in conflict is power and the dynamics of power. The questions are often:

"Am I up or am I down?"

"Who gets to say what counts here?"

"Will I be able to influence and get my needs met, my interests satisfied?"

"Can we all be powerful, or if you are powerful, can I be powerful too?"

"Can I have my 'no' and still have connection and relationship with you?"

"Can I have my autonomy without fear of attack?"

"If I step forward, will I be shamed and belittled?"

"Will this group idolize then kill the leader?"

There are many group themes that influence the way we unconsciously relate to others and ourselves. Hidden influences to expose and explore the power dynamics in groups can include: Education, race, gender/ body, sexual orientation, spiritual training, social class (rank, power, and privilege), money, geography, encounters with the legal system, mental illness (and addictions), family (secrets, cut-offs, adoption), members of cults. These themes can make us feel consciously or unconsciously superior/entitled or marginalized. By unconsciously accepting these themes, we limit our access to a direct experience of our true nature, value and worth as human beings.

When we are not in our power, or are holding back from engaging in working through our differences, we can get stuck in cycles of conflict that don't move our mutual creativity forward. The basic unhelpful conflict styles are: Ignore, withdraw, deflect, accommodate, escalate, compromise, compete, and collaborate. In MatrixWorks, the following points outline our approach to the theme of conflict:

1) We are choosing to reframe a conventional understanding of conflict in these ways
   a) Reframing conflict as doorway to creativity
   b) Reframing conflict as training in the capacity to notice, name and work with differences as gifts
   c) Reframing power as potency
2) Uncouple conflict from trauma
3) Couple conflict with relationship: conflict is essential to move relationship past stuck places. Staying in connection and relationship through conflict is essential in order to deepen our capacity to grow together.
4) Understanding working with conflict as a primary liberator of energy.
5) Letting go of fear and avoidance of conflict allows us to live with more love and connection.
6) Accepting the Four "F's" as gifts of working with this stage: freedom, fearlessness, formlessness, and flexibility. We claim the freedom to be more of who we are. We experience the flexibility of being able to shift our position from rigidity and fixedness to openness and possibility. We cultivate fearlessness by staying with the conflict until 'something else (the higher third) happens'. We embody formlessness by allowing the energy of conflict to dissolve and reform in healthy ways.

So, to explore this domain, we have to broaden our perceptions to include a deeper exploration of roles, including stereotypes and archetypes. We need to look at issues of rank, privilege, and power. We need to look at all the ways the Matrix can be distorted by invisible, unnamed issues of power. We need to invite what is in the underbelly to come forward. We need to name and welcome the taboos into greater awareness.

Roles are universal functions (e.g. mother, child, worker, teacher, trouble-maker, etc.) that individuals play out in groups. Roles can become stereotypes and archetypes. If and when this happens, we have lost the person and only see the role. We see these archetypes played out by polarities, for example, liberals versus conservatives, East coast versus West coast, science versus spirituality. An archetype is a universal energy pattern. In groups, at the conflict stage, archetypes 'fly' around looking for a person to attach to and work through. Without awareness, we can begin to 'act out' feelings that do not belong to us at all.

We accept that stereotypes, archetypes and polarities are part of the group field territory. But we recognize them in order to transcend them. Contrast a group that welcomes differences, with a group that works with differences through scapegoating, banishing, punishing and shaming. Becoming more conscious of this phenomenon helps us avoid the pitfalls of this more primitive way of working with these powerful energies.

Let's look at some examples of natural role tensions: In business we find this between design and marketing. The alternative community prefers alternative medicine and the mainstream community more traditional medicine. In education we find a polarity between academics and arts. In politics, we have the republicans and democrats. The truth is each holds part of the truth. How can we build bridges that connect the wisdom of both sides, rather than polarize and fight holy wars? What would it be like to cultivate a world where everyone is right? A thesis and antithesis is unfinished without the satisfaction of a synthesis.

The key to making Chaos/Conflict an experience of excitement and a liberation of energy is to stay in relationship through the exploration. If I am truly committed to the relationship and trust that something can emerge that satisfies both of our needs, then, the experience of working with conflict is exhilarating.

The rewards are enormous. In this approach, right use of power is possible. In MatrixWorks, we believe that our survival as a species depends on learning to work with conflict in this way. And, we see the MatrixWorks Training as a practice field for learning more about this way of working with conflict and chaos. Conflict takes us to deeper and deeper levels of inclusion.

At the most outer and simple level, we see conflict as having opposing parts: a yes and a no. However, if we shift perceptions and look more deeply at an inner level, we experience the power of paradox, the tension and connection of opposites. And, if we can open to a still deeper level, the 'secret' level, where awareness is big enough to see the whole, the conflict dissolves. This level is beyond our thinking mind and can't be forced or pretended. It often appears as grace and support for our full humanness.

Resources for Working with Conflict:

- Get the other's personal story and communicate that you got it. Be willing to wait for resolution to emerge.
- Be willing to accept resolution may not occur.
- Couple a complaint with a request for change.
- Hold your seat.
- Take a stand and be willing to yield
- Enlist and engage a subgroup.
- Commit to using conflict to get closer, deeper, or clearer.
- Uncouple conflict from trauma.
- Learn when to persist and when to let go.
- Be curious.
- Pay attention to the three levels: personal, interpersonal, and group.
- Express sorrow and make amends.
- Remember your resilience.
- Move from explaining to exploring and make the implicit explicit.

Perturbance
The Art of Gentle Disturbance

A leader or facilitator cannot command and control a group. While leaders do try this method, the intended outcome over time won't align with the actual result. Like a garden, we can only set the conditions for nature to work its magic. To set the conditions for a group to come alive, we can nudge and cajole. Using a living systems model of understanding groups, only two kinds of interventions are possible:

1: Operate on the *principle of containment* and provide the function of safety. In the early stages of facilitation when the group is just forming, it is essential that at least 70-80 percent of interventions are of the principle of containment.

2: Intervene with the *capacity for perturbation* and insert a challenge or the possibility for confrontation into the field of the group. This end of the spectrum should be used very sparingly at the beginning of the group. At each of the phases, systematically perturbing the group to evolve forward is a part of the facilitator's toolkit.

The ability to alternate interventions that are containing in nature and those that are perturbing in nature is an essential part of the learning trajectory. If you try to perturb a group, before safety is established, you've created a problem. On the other hand, if you fail to perturb a group after safety is established, you've missed an opportunity for growth and development.

In the early days of teaching MatrixWorks, there was some pretty wild chaos. During one eight-day immersion class in Brazil, people were assigned to safety groups for the first two days. The groups were well functioning and everything was going smoothly. On the third day, we dissolved the groups and had the participants chose new groups, which perturbed unifying archetypes and a sense of *"I'm not chosen, I'm not wanted."* Feelings of threat were activated in the group members during this shift. One woman wanted to be in group A, but group B and C also wanted her. So I egged people on to perturb the group: "who's going to get to decide here? Do you care enough to make it happen your way?" Members of group B went over to group A and actually picked her up to steal her for their group, and everyone was activated. She was both delighted and frozen. Group A said they'd been robbed. Group C said they felt like the losers because they didn't even get the chance to have her.

Maybe I'm too dumb to be afraid, because my co-facilitator was shaking her head. I had everyone sit down and asked the woman at the center of the conflict, "how is this for you?" She started to cry, and shared: "I was never wanted. I was never chosen. That people would fight to have me in their group, it was the missing experience for me." The magical moment of chaos and what looked like extreme volatility was actually a deep unwinding of a healing experience. The group was able to feel and experience the concept that chaos is the evolutionary impulse for healing. In these moments of openness, we touch a direct experience of one thing falling apart and something else coming together. Acting out and then pausing to become mindful, rewrote the script for this woman's life. It rewrote the script for this group. I couldn't have known that, I only tried to amplify it by bringing out the chaos. If you don't go from the outer level of chaos to the inner level of what's happening underneath, you miss the point. The group's unconscious was helping her have the experience, and her healing affected all the players in the group. The purpose was not for groups to be figured out but for that process to unfold.

With enough experience you come to trust even the clumsiest difficult things and know something else is running the show. I can't know but I can become more sensitive and I can trust even the most absurd situations. Wherever there's fire, it's the evolutionary impulse trying to set the conditions for next level of growth and healing trying to happen. Nothing to do but bow to that intelligence that knows, allowing and trusting that the healing impulse is always looking for an opportunity to express itself.

Intention and Impact
Relationship is all there is

O f all of the tools of MatrixWorks that have been used in many different contexts, I think the particular tool of knowing how to work with intention and impact is one of the most powerful lenses through which to see everything. Intention is really synonymous with a goal, it's what I'm orienting towards (e.g. my intention with this team is to foster trust and creativity), and impact is what happens when I try to implement what I'm wanting. It's the result of the aim.

Sometimes our intention and impact don't match up in the way we want. An arrow doesn't reach the target, and we can't control the impact of where it lands. What I'm suggesting is that the person who receives the aim, not the person who initiates the aim, defines the result. I get to say the intention; you get to say the impact.

This process levels the playing field and makes 'right and wrong' more relational. And for most organizations that I've worked with (the large organizations, middle management, and high-level leaders), once they really get this and make it a practice to view things in this way, it changes everything. It allows us to both be right and allows us to include ourselves in the equation.

One of the most common examples of seeing the usefulness of this tool is managing expectations and agreements. Let's say for example I have an agreement to turn in my part of the group project on Wednesday. Something happens and I have an emergency and I don't deliver on my intention. I've trained myself to understand that things happen, but to care about this change and what impact it has on you. I know my intentions were good, but the intended result just didn't happen. Caring about the impact instead of making excuses, I might say: "my intention was to get

116

this to you, but because of this reason I'm not able to deliver, and I care about the impact on you and how it may make things more difficult." The shift in my perspective to include the impact of the other starts to build more trust and more strength in the relational field. In contrast, what we often see in groups that haven't yet reached a level of synergy is a one-sided explanation: "I just can't do it." When the conversation stops there, then it leaves out a whole other world of what's affected and negates feelings of the other. This results in a breach of trust. To help things run smoothly, we must be able to include both people and both sides of the situation, giving people the benefit of the doubt around intention: "I know your intention was to get the project to me and the impact on me was quite serious." So knowing how to separate the intention from the impact, knowing that they can be different, and including both of those worldviews will result in better communication, and less unnecessary conflict. By working in this way I am making a choice to believe that people are doing the best that they can.

Practice: Intention and impact

I am responsible for my Intentions
You are responsible for the impact on you

We are skillful in relationship when Intention and Impact are aligned--when they match

We have problems in relationship when there is a gap between Intention and Impact.

Reverse roles and repeat exercise

"My intention with _____ is _____." "I imagine my impact is_____."

"Please give me Feedback on how my Intention and Impact could be better aligned"

Reverse roles and repeat exercise

Shadow and Shine: 3, 2, 1, 0 Process

(Adapted from Integral Theory Life Practice and personal study with Diane Hamilton, Zen Teacher)

"Shadow has us believe we will not prosper from doing things we most love." -R. Rudd

A crucial aspect of our commitment to keep 'Growing-Up' as human beings is a willingness to explore the parts of us that we disown, reject, repress, deny or, are simply not conscious of. In other words, *our SHADOW parts.*

In this simple 3, 2, 1, 0 process, we learn how to identify a person, situation, or event that is disturbing us and work with it so that we can re-integrate the aspect of ourselves we have projected onto the person, situation, or event. The key aspect of the power of the process is moving through the perspectives of 3rd Person, 2nd Person and 1st Person. The following is a template for working with this approach. Work is done in partners.

Step 1: Partner A: Name something that is irritating you about _____. Let's say something about the MatrixWorks class that is annoying you. You then speak or write about this without holding back. You have a free pass to complain completely about Us, It, that Thing. This is the 3rd Person Perspective. It is important to really go for it and in a way, discharge some energy. If writing, take 5-8 minutes. If speaking, take 3-5 minutes. Partner B listens, encourages Partner A and reflects back understanding in simple phrases. This phase of the process is very energetic and the whole room will be very alive. Time: 10-15 minutes

Step 2: Now, the shift to 2nd Person Perspective is engaged. Partner B takes on the role of what Partner A is upset about. Partner A then talks directly to Partner B. What is important here is that we are entering into relationship with what has annoyed and disturbs us. We are bringing it closer to us, and having a conversation with our disturbance. Something usually starts to shift at this step because the process is more intimate and personal. Time: 7-10 minutes

Step 3: Now, the shift is to 1st person and Partner A begins to be curious about how this disturbance is a part of himself. Partner A sees more deeply into the source of frustration and irritation. Instead of projecting all the feelings out on the situation, Partner A has the capacity to self-reflect and re-claim the projections. Partner A shares with Partner B the insights and energetic shifts that are happening. Together they explore what Gift would come from integrating the Shadow piece that has been worked with. They may explore the polarities that have been present in the Shadow work. At this stage there is often the feeling of genuine compassion and understanding for self and other. Both Partners can experience a kind of new SHINE from the honesty of reclaiming Shadow. Time: 10-15 minutes

Step 4: Sitting in silence, both Partners rest their awareness in Big Mind/Big Heart and hold the whole process with spacious compassion. Share appreciations as they are felt. *Then reverse roles and repeat the process.*

Reflection questions: what is your relationship to this template of intention and impact? In what aspects of your work and your life do you feel like your intention and impact are in alignment, and where is there a mismatch? Where do you get feedback from your community that your intention and your impact don't match? Choose three people in your life, and do the intention impact exercise with them if they are willing, and ask for feedback. What needs to change so my intention and impact on you can be more in alignment?

Feedback
The Food for Living Systems

Feedback is an essential tool for broadening our capacity to include the perspective of the other. An ability to include multiple perspectives is essential for working in a living systems way. To create life-affirming groups, organizations, and relationships, we have to be willing to ask for, receive, and work with a process of feedback. Feedback is the mechanism for bringing intention and impact closer together. As an example, my intention is to teach MatrixWorks, but I have to be in relationship with my audience to know if it is actually helping, so I know the impact. I can't say it's my intention to teach it so therefore you're learning it. That power is in your hands. Feedback allows for a shift in communication and behavior so that intent and impact can be closer together. Feedback is an essential part in how we make our intentions useful for other people.

Learning how to give and receive Feedback is a skill and an art. Ideally it helps us to self-correct. Feedback is essential to healthy individuals and group functioning. It informs us whether our intentions match our impact. It illuminates blind spots and develops an ever-increasing awareness about how we are in relationship.

Feedback is about sharing information and contains a request for a change. Most of us have been conditioned to think feedback is critical. What if we unlearn this pattern and approach feedback as if it were a gift? In living systems, feedback is food for the group. Here are some ideas about giving feedback:

FEEDBACK EXERCISE
"Tell me an effect I have on you."

Feedback is essential 'food for living systems.' Without this food, we as individuals are not able to realize our potential as individuals or groups. This exercise is designed to provide 'food' and teach us how to 'grow food.'

Structure: Done in pairs. Repeat with all the group members.

1. Person A

"As I sit here with you now, I notice what arises in me. . . I am drawn to . . ." (about the self)

"When I let that impact/affect me, I feel, imagine, think or sense..." (about the other)

"Then I get curious and wonder about . . ." (about the relationship between you)

For example: I want to smile...I start to feel warmth in me...I wonder what it would be like to work together. Moving from me, to you, to us.

Person B says "Thank you"
Repeat the process one more time.

2. Person B says the phrases above and Person A says "Thank you." Repeat the process one more time.

Take five minutes at the end to sit in silence with each other and notice the impact of this exercise on your sense of yourself, connection to 'other' and connection to something larger.

3. Debrief as partners

Archetypes
Group Roles and Dynamics

Maturity is the ability to find the similarities in the apparently different, and the differences between the apparently similar. The goal is to differentiate and then integrate these differences.
-Ivonne Agarzarian

Knowing who we are in groups is just as important as knowing about ourselves. And understanding how we show up in groups gives us insight into how we might try something new, outside the box and into the freedom of authentic relationship. There are universal energies, or archetypes that predominate group roles and help us see what part we are playing. When we claim our own archetype we gain the freedom to truly express ourselves. Polarities, archetypes, scapegoating, and victimhood all give us tools and insights into how to facilitate paradigm shifts in our lives, our work, and our world.

Polarities

Polarities represent the relationship between opposite forces. They can show up as oppositional, understanding, or accepting of a creative tension. When acknowledged, polarities help groups explore the spectrum of diverse gifts members bring. The goal of exposing polarities is to uncover the highest wisdom that can hold both ends of the spectrum. Body systems come in polarities: fluids and bones, structure and flow, process and output, inhale and exhale. When a group is stuck, the body systems can function as a diagnostic tool to bring the group back to health. As Dan Siegel says, health is the integration of differentiated parts. So, when a group is frozen, it's because there's no movement or communication between the opposing poles.

Polarities are a natural part of chaos. Once there's enough safety, the group is ready to move naturally into creative chaos. Members need to be safe enough to risk sharing themselves. Preferences and predispositions show up as resistance, and they are a good indication that the group needs to be perturbed by the facilitator.

Polarities are important because we often learn by contrast. For example: I learn about expansion by experiencing both expansion and contraction. If I only experience one side of a pole, then I don't have much freedom or perspective. Conflict arises because people are attached to one side of a pole and can't see an upside of the opposite. We also tend not to see the downsides and shadow of our own side. Prior conditioning (i.e. the need to be right, the need to maintain one's own perspective at the expense of the other) can predispose us to close-mindedness. Staying stuck in a pole results in the inability to take on another's perspective, and ultimately inhibits growth and evolution.

Being able to identify, to track and name the polarities in each particular group is fundamental to facilitation mastery. It also serves as a helpful diagnostic tool. Tracking what polarities are flowing and which are stuck is a skillful facilitation practice. A skillful facilitator will point the group towards what contributes to wholeness, while identifying where the parts get paralyzed in frozen poles. The goal is right relationship with both sides.

A paradigm is something that serves as a pattern or a model of how things work in the world. Paradigm shifts are a fundamental change in view of how things work/should work.

Polarities in right relationship create the paradox that allows for paradigm shift; stuck polarities keep the paradigm stuck. Life requires polarities: to stay living I have to stay in difference and allow for the higher 3rd to emerge.

From Problems	**To** Possibilities
Scarcity	Abundance
Problem – driven	Vision-led
Resistance	Generative Thinking
Competing with others	Collaborating
Command/Control	Nudge and Cajole for self-direction
Money	Energy
Critical Analysis	Meaning
Incremental changes	Breakthroughs
Transactions	Relationships
Linearity	Serendipity
Push	Pull
Map	Compass
Solidity	Process
Me vs. We	MWe
Hierarchy	Networks

Archetypes

The way I use archetypes is pointing to a universal energy of how we show up in groups. For example, I'm a mother, but when I invoke the divine mother I move from the personal to the subtle universal larger energy. When I change perspectives to the divine mother, it's not so personal, its more universal. This is a fluid approach to understanding larger forces of energy. All the most powerful ideas in history go back to archetypes of self, shadow, animas, and persona. What we're trying to do is link the person and their sense of empowerment to this larger energy to find it in themselves as a beautiful integration of personal and universal.

We first work with polarities to establish a field of opposites. When we work with polarities and choosing, we open a field that has archetypes in it. The exercise we do is set up to help people discover what is their anchor into goodness and truth, those things that hold us in the place we want to be. The archetype exercise is a self-discovery process, leaving each member with a symbol they can hold when pulled into opposing forces. Archetypes also serve as the armor and protection that keeps us from being pulled into the scapegoat archetype. This relates back to the concept of living systems in that all parts are essential to the whole of the system, and being able to connect to the whole gives us a greater appreciation for all of the parts, even when there are differences. We want to be able to operate in the field of the personal, but also in the transpersonal and universal, and archetypes pull them all together.

Usually we offer the archetype exercise after we've explored the integration of love and power and the many aspects of confused chaos. This exercise is a way for people to claim their power while staying in relationship. It is conducted in small groups with feedback from the people in the groups.

Archetype Exercise:

This exercise can be done in small groups of two to four people. The small groups choose the roles of experiencer, guide, and supporter(s), chosen by the experiencer. The guide asks the experiencer a series of questions. With each question, the experiencer takes a step forward, and then the guide and supporter(s) follow along next to the experiencer. The experiencer pauses at each step to reflect deeply on the question.

1. Name a power you have, something you feel confident in, a potency you have (*examples: curiosity, intuition, energy, consciousness, awareness, playfulness, strength*).

2. Name a quality or qualities you possess (*examples: catalyst, loving, patient, friendly, open, sensitive, wise, thoughtful, reliable*).

---

3. Name roles that are important to you (*examples: leader, supporter, nourisher, teacher, sister, friend, lone wolf, facilitator*).

4. What have you been told is the dark side of these roles, qualities, and powers? (*examples: troublemaker, loudmouth, negative, careless, impatient, selfish, vague, dumb*).

5. Is there a unifying energy that runs through all of these, that represents the deepest truth about you? (*Guide and supporters can offer reflections without projecting or pushing them onto the experiencer. The experiencer will claim their power and name here*). Is there a name for your archetypal energy? (*The experiencer states the name. Examples: Eve, Hestia, Nourishing Devotee, Warrior Priestess, Star, and Hummingbird. The possibilities are endless*). How does your archetype relate to your calling in the world? How might your archetype relate differently to your obstacles? Do you feel empowered?

My archetype might play out this way: *I have the power of being interested in consciousness because it gives me energy. I am a person who loves to be a rascal, bringing forth the first step into the second step. My roles are to be a good friend, to teach in a way that people learn to become leaders. I've been told I'm a troublemaker, I've asked myself why I can't just keep quiet, to open door for negative archetypes to become more conscious and integrated and accepted. My archetypes name is divine play.*

When the experiencer has claimed a name for their personal archetype, the guide then asks the experiencer to answer the same questions in reverse order, stepping back along the same path for each question, but this time answering as the archetype. At the end, the experiencer now integrates their original self with their archetypal energy.

If there's a unifying energy that runs through all of these things that represents the deepest truth about you right now in this moment. The guide and supporter can help refine this. (Example: The energy that's a deep truth about me is I'm a creator. I like to create. And I can own this truth to ground me.) Holding onto that deeper truth, answer questions: how does your archetype relate to your calling in the world (Ex: I want to create a new and innovative way of working with groups). There's something about the claiming that allows us to self-recognize the energy trying to manifest instead of taking on other's projections of me. It's very empowering. Do you feel empowered? Group sharing of archetypes to welcome these powerful energies into the group with love.

Supports self-recognition, supports empowerment, and gives a counter-balance to the scapegoat. The archetype becomes a guardian to protect against the scapegoat. There's something that happens when we support others through this process with another and then when we go through chaos in the future it helps us see their light.

Scapegoating

The theme of the scapegoat goes all the way back to biblical times, when Aaron scarified a goat for God. The scapegoat also has roots in ancient Greece where the community would cast out a lower member of society to represent purification of the community. One was a higher sacrifice and one was banishment, but either way, scapegoating doesn't feel great for the castaway, nor does it accomplish what we intend. We understand this in modern psychological terms as the tendency of a group to cast out a member who may represent a source of blame. This is a factor of projection or displacement of uncomfortable feelings, which we assign to others instead of processing within ourselves. It is a way not to own our own shadows, whether individually or as part of a group.

When a group doesn't accept all the parts of itself, scapegoating can occur. We all carry both shadows and light, and this is true at the level of the group. When we don't process our shadows, they rule us unconsciously. Scapegoating is the dis-integration of what the group considers "negative archetypes." The idea that I can purify myself by banishing another with my sins keeps the group (or individual) in a holding pattern of chaos.

The scapegoat is an archetypal energy that gets projected onto a person. It cannot be resolved be casting out that person, because the energy still remains in the system, unprocessed. If you remove the scapegoat, the energy will still look for another to attach to. In groups, when one person is fired or moves on, then the next most disconnected person from the matrix steps in and starts creating the same problems. If scapegoating is active, the system isn't seeing itself and it is distorted from the whole. The scapegoat locks us into the duality of right and wrong, blocking the energy of creativity and transformation.

If the scapegoat archetype is active, call it to everyone's attention. Pause, practice mindfulness, be curious, and inquire what is going on behind the objects to see the system. The healing impulse wants to integrate all parts by seeing alternate solutions. It's really the system trying to make itself whole. The next section shares a tool for transforming the scapegoat archetype and unleashing group genius.

In MatrixWorks, we bring an understanding of this archetypal pattern to the forefront of group awareness, so that a group may come to understand this tendency, and find new tools to work with it.

Shifting from Victim to Creator

The empowerment triangle, developed by David Emerald, gives groups a healthy way of working with scapegoating. It's the alternative to the drama triangle (see figures below), offering a way of seeing negative dynamics that makes it easier to work with and transform.

The empowerment triangle turns drama upside-down, transforming the persecutor (or scapegoat) into a challenger, the rescuer into a coach, and the victim into a creator. The empowerment dynamic allows all the roles to be essential for growth.

In the drama triangle, the persecutor works with issues of power, the rescuer works with issues of responsibility, and the victim works with area of vulnerability:

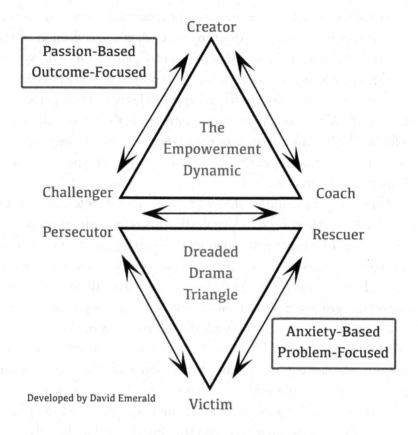

Developed by David Emerald

The drama triangle is familiar to many of us. We all know this pattern inside ourselves. We get stuck in a situation that we want to escape, and it creates drama. By leaning into the dynamic and entering deeper into relationship, we can work the energy so that it becomes an enriching transformation. If you can work this in a group, then you've subdued the scapegoat archetype and turned it into something more life affirming.

The most important thing about the drama triangle is to make people aware of it. When a group can understand and recognize how this is a kind of destructive pattern, it becomes empowered to change the pattern. Uncoupling drama from our organizational and personal lives is the key. The group as a whole can embody a role to create safety and make sense of the system.

Transformation from the drama to the redeemed starts with a pause, then an inquiry of what's happening here, then a recollection of the three roles and who is playing what role in this context. Once the system is self-aware, ask the questions: "what else is possible? How can I become so centered that something new can happen? How can a new perception take place?" With enough safety and connection, the group will be able to follow the healing energy into re-organization and re-integration of the parts. Claiming or remembering your own archetype can protect against falling into one.

I once taught a workshop to a very sophisticated professional group of about 35 people in Brazil. I love the Brazilians for their expressiveness and culture. I had split this group into three subgroups and led them through the process of connection and chaos. As we were entering into the final session on creative evolution (which I also call consciousness), one of the groups exploded into conflict. These sophisticated and professional stars started throwing things, running out of the room, and cursing each other. They were as expressive as anything I'd ever seen. On the last day of training, I met with a conflict pair that was spitting insults at each other, and none of my interventions with this pair changed anything. So after all of my attempts, I told the pair "I quit," and I really did step back into trusting the healing impulse.

Needing to complete the session, we moved ahead as planned with each of the groups doing their final presentation. The first and second groups went, and when it was time for the last group to go, the whole room could feel the mean vibes of their hatred for one another. One woman in the final group stood up to present, but instead of going forward with what the group had prepared, she started singing the word "connection" over and over to the tune of "frarajaca." Her singing and movements were so loud and boisterous that they began to change the dynamic of the group's energy. One at a time, she held out her hands to both of the members of the conflict pair, and they joined in, eventually inviting their whole subgroup and then the rest of the participants. By the end of the class, everyone in the room was singing and dancing and crying and laughing in connection. All of a sudden, the love in the room has been transformed and restored.

I had truly let go knowing I had done my best in the situation, and when nothing else had worked, the Brazilians will sing and dance. The moment when healing peaks through is the moment of new creation. This begins the next cycle and turning of the wheel in connection, chaos, and creative evolution. You can't do anything to make it happen, but it's always there. The more I remember[11] it, the more I can offer myself to it.

Practice: Consider patterns of roles and dynamics in your relationships, groups, and organizations. What patterns do they get captured by? What role do you play? What's the effect of these roles and dynamics? How did you help to create these patterns? How can you work with these roles to bring about more creativity? How can we work together to create a new reality?

Creative Evolution
The Emergence of New Possibilities when Opposites Unite

"Licking honey from the Razor's Edge"
"Have you been loved enough?"
"Can we know the world as womb and the womb as world?"

These invitations orient us to our third phase of the group life cycle. This emergence is the most deeply personal and rewarding of the stages. Following connection and chaos, creative evolution is when we taste the ripened 'fruit' of the work. The depth of healing arises for each individual and for the community. In our first class on inclusion, we begin laying down the lines of connection and invited the personal and interpersonal to manifest. In the second class on chaos and conflict, we run energy through the lines of connection and open the door to universal energies and archetypes. We liberate lively, creative energy. However, it is in the third class that the personal/particular and universal energies come together and re-combine to fully call forth the new individual that is both human and divine. In this class we move through the spaces between the lines of the Matrix and find each other and ourselves in new ways. Working with consciousness and awareness is the result of being able to connect while staying in dynamic relationship during conflict.

At this stage of a group's life, we have the possibility to re-encounter a matrix of connection and bond more deeply with our true nature and each other. In this state, the truth of non-separateness is available as a direct experience. Once we have cultivated enough loving-kindness, compassion, appreciation, and equanimity, we radiate into our lives and groups the power to create life-affirming work. When we move from awareness of a contained self to connection with all life, we receive the benefits of greater wholeness of being.

For this reason, in the Mutual Connection class, we begin to look more deeply into our patterning from our family of origin, from our membership in spiritual and professional communities. We risk opening to new possibilities and a new life that is more aligned with the truth of who we are, with the truth of our human condition – Universal and Personal, Absolute and Relative, Mutual and Transpersonal.

We can wake up to the promise of relationships that are grounded in Mutual and Transpersonal Connection. Our deepest human need for Mutual and Transpersonal Connection is within reach and is more essential than ever for this time in history.

It is our deepest hope that the strength of our connections – mutual and transpersonal – will support us to let go of the fears that cause our suffering and restore in us a deep confidence in our original nature.

Practice: Enactment Labs.

Having experimented with this process in many classes, we find they are useful regardless of the theme of the class. Enactment Labs deepen the experience of transformation for individuals and for groups. The theory and content of the class comes alive as we practice our Enactment Labs. Here is a brief description of the process.

A MatrixWorks participant chooses to work on a situation, a difficulty, or a problem. The basic structure of the process is that there is a Protagonist (the MatrixWorks participant) and then 2-5 other group members' stand-in for these roles/functions:

1. The goal or desire the Protagonist is trying to achieve or accomplish.

2. The obstacle or force preventing the Protagonist from reaching his/her goal.
3. An ally who is supporting the Protagonist through out the process
4. Other roles may be added as the process unfolds.

After roles are assigned, we begin exploring experientially 'the new possibility that wants to happen'. We begin a deep dive into spontaneity, risk taking, and high play. We welcome transformative surprises and listen deeply to the whispers of both body and soul as unbounded creativity and healing enter into our space. Through this process of the Enactment Lab, we have the opportunity to serve new life, and taste greater fulfillment in our human experience.

Once the dynamic process is complete, we engage in a whole group de-brief and share about our learnings and the impact of the process. It is our intention that each person in a MatrixWorks class has the opportunity to do an Enactment Lab, if they choose.

One enactment lab in particular stands out. At one of my trainings in Japan, a very gentle man with what I would characterize as cultivation and refinement in his energy, did an enactment about wanting more contact and the ability to reach out. He was an advanced cranio-sacral teacher that understood the subtle energy in the body. We set up his enactment with people representing the kind of contact that he wanted to have, then we played with holding him back as he experienced wanting to fully reach, creating resistance to his longing to reach out. It was quite powerful for him to experience this wanting. Then we experimented with the other part of the polarity. He was holding himself back, and we were pulling his arms out to reach so he could experience what it was like to hold back, and eventually collapsed into the arms of his friend and made a beautiful statement *"I've been longing for the truth of this connection"*.

It was quite an emotional experience for him, and at the end his physical expression was so much more embodied in refinement and level of cultivation, a quality of exquisite gentleness. And I'll never forget he looked at me and there was a long period of eye contact and then he said these words *"I feel as if I have embodied my soul"* and I looked at him and realized that is what I could see: that his spirit had found a level of integration that allowed all the parts of him to fit together into a convergent whole.

To summarize, enactments simplify the elements to reach the bare bones of what is happening for the person. Finding a way to physicalize the pinch point, and working with it like taffy, massages the muscle of change until something new emerges. The healing impulse gives new life to the full capacity for expression. From this state, the inner capacity and outer expression are more congruent. Enactments generate an increased harmony between the inner experience of consciousness and the outer expression with the environment.

Reflection questions: Name 3 scenarios for you personally that you feel like you could do an enactment with, elements of you, something you want, and obstacle.

Of those 3, choose one and write out how this might work. What would you say is the challenge, the goal, the obstacle, and how might this benefit your life? Option to embody the characters in your writing.

Part Three
The Fruit: Practical Application

Going Forth in a VUCA World
The Calling of Our Times

We have a heart disease epidemic in this country: not only physical heart disease, but emotional and spiritual heart disease from profound feelings of loneliness, isolation, alienation and depression from the breakdown of social structures that have provided us with a sense of connection and community. The lack of connection and community, is, to me, the root of all illness, cynicism and violence in our society.
- Dean Ornish

Fruit is transformation. It's the embodiment of vision. It's abundance. The quality of the fruit is ripe, alive, nourishing. When the ground and the path merge into fruit, it makes doing more natural. Because in the natural great perfection the fruit is already there, it's already done. We just have to relax into the flow.

To illustrate this notion, I'll share a few words about that path of the Buddha. The Buddha was a human being, like us. And, like many of us he had privilege: a very good life--many people to care for him. He had many 'mothers' taking care of him. He was set to be the ruler of the Kingdom and was protected from all problems of life. As the story goes, he became curious about what the world was like outside of the Castle, so he convinced one of his servants to take him out. Once out in the world he saw sick people in Pain. When he asked what this was, he was told "This is Sickness". Then he saw someone who had died and was told "This is Death". Next he saw very old people, crippled and walking with canes and was told "This is Aging". Finally, he saw a woman giving birth and heard the cries of Labor and was told "This is the pain of Birth". The servant then told him that Birth, Death, Sickness and Old Age happen to everyone. The Buddha then cried and vowed to find a way out of Suffering. This is the subject of our endeavors. How we can become free of unnecessary suffering--the suffering about suffering.

When Buddha reached enlightenment, his first teaching was about the four noble truths. The First Noble Truth is that suffering exists. The Second Noble Truth is that suffering is caused by desire for things to be different than they are , and ignorance of how things really are. The Third Noble Truth is that suffering can end at any time when we let go of desire, ill will, and ignorance. The Fourth Noble Truth is that life is fruitful when we walk the middle path between extremes. This is the liberation from polarities.

Like the Time of the Buddha over 2500 years ago, the kind of world we are living in now is a world of suffering. The military refers to our current conditions as VUCA[12] (volatile, uncertain, complex, and ambiguous). This world makes it hard for us to receive what Rick Hanson describes as our fundamental human needs: safety, satisfaction, and connection.

We suffer whenever we want things to be different than how they are. When our fundamental needs are not met, we experience ignorance and suffering, putting us into an emotionally reactive mode. We can learn to be free of suffering by cultivating safety, satisfaction, and connection. Rick Hanson advises us to take in the good through small amounts of focus and time that allow us to install new structures in the brain.

We can use VUCA as the fuel for transformation by knowing the situational context, and connecting to a knowing that something else is possible. All groups have messiness—you just need skills to be a human being in relationship. It's not easy—it takes time, patience, and collaboration. Working with the exercises in this book towards becoming a living matrix has helped many groups become responsive to evolutionary intelligence instead of being caught up in reactivity.

When we have safety, satisfaction, and connection, we are in a responsive mode, which means we have choice. When we experience a lack or deficit of these fundamental needs, we become emotionally reactive, which means we have no choice.

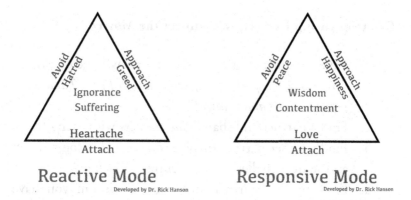

Reactive Mode

Developed by Dr. Rick Hanson

Responsive Mode

Developed by Dr. Rick Hanson

The freedom of wisdom and contentment becomes available through these four keys: Recognize, resource, regulate, and relate.

- Recognize the trigger. Pause to remove yourself from the situation and reflect on how you feel. Recognize the ways in which your heart may be closed, your amygdala is hijacked, and you may be building a case against the person or situation.
- Resource yourself by providing some self-nourishment (go for a walk, practice yoga, meditate for a few minutes, cuddle your dog, choose any of the practices or maps from this book to self-regulate).
- Regulate the situation by spending energy in peace-making.
- Relate by sharing your experience, being open to feedback, and creating new intention for building the relationship.

When we add this information to what we are learning about neuroscience, we understand even more deeply why learning new ways of being in groups and relationships of mutuality are so vital.

In our MatrixWorks Training, we are exploring a template for groups as living systems that is based on love, connection and support. We are learning to live in a relational field where we use our "smart social nervous system" and let love and an openness of heart be the ground we rest in, be the ground we are.

Practice: Group Exercise to Connect the Matrix

1. Take a moment with yourself and answer the questions: *"How do you experience suffering in your life? What are you ready to learn and change?"*
2. Find a partner and share your answers with each other.
3. Find another partner (maybe someone you don't know) and share a challenge you're currently facing.
4. Find another partner and share a wisdom you have learned from your own suffering. Share something you are still learning from your own suffering.
5. Share as a whole group.

Practice: The Inner Side of Leadership. Working alone, journal about the following questions:

1. What are 3 challenges you currently face in your work, or life?
2. What are your current most vital sources of Love and energy (work and/or life)
3. What is trying to emerge or be born in you at this time?
4. What needs to die, to be let go of, so that the new can emerge in you

Reflection Questions: Reflect on the areas of your life where you are reactive and where you are responsive. Are you willing to work toward becoming more responsive?[13]

21ˢᵗ Century Organizations

2 1ˢᵗ century leadership is so complex that awareness and consciousness are like oxygen: vital nutrients for it to breathe and function properly. Like the messes I created in groups when I was young, our organizations, governments, and industries have created a lot of modern messes. As individualistic humans and corporations, we have gone astray from harmony with the Earth and each other. To clean up our messes, we need to work in a way that increases awareness, consciousness, and life itself. We are practicing finding the higher fusion of polarities, and creating a world where the temple and the marketplace are one in the same. When companies start to work this way, there's an energetic shift from competition to common intention that allows us to be better together.

Companies with consciousness are looking at how to unleash human potential. In companies working to adopt a non-hierarchical model, whenever someone is having poor performance, I ask him or her to stop focusing on work and focus on what's happening in their life. Moving to a more personal and dynamic relationship inevitably made their work soar again.

We can unleash human potential and make the environment human friendly by igniting the 5 friends and safety, satisfaction, and connection. We can no longer separate the personal from the workplace and still have health and creativity.

In our 21ˢᵗ century organizations and quest for leadership models, we need to look for models that allow leadership itself to evolve, and this evolution harvests the fruit of each persons gifts. When we keep practicing inclusion of whatever has been marginalized, we then become better able to perceive and live from the whole, rather than the part.

Leadership Qualities

Great suffering exists in all pockets of the globe. In order to respond to this need for healing, our societies need stronger communities and networks, our communities need stronger tribes and teams, our teams rely on strong individuals, individuals must connect with themselves. Enlightened Feminine energy is critical in Leadership during this time in history. If we are to thrive as a species, we must learn to work together with more care, compassion and creativity by putting Love back into Leadership.

The essence of the teachings of the Buddha offers us wisdom for leading the emerging future. After studying many extreme approaches, the Buddha came to what is called "the middle way," which is not extreme. The Buddha as a teacher was a healer. He saw the disease and he recommended a cure. This means taking responsibility for our thoughts, actions, speech, relationships, body, mind, livelihood, intentions, business, concentration etc., etc. In the Middle Way, the main message of the cure is we must take responsibility for all aspects of our lives. When we commit to this way of living, we begin to end unnecessary suffering; the Suffering about Suffering and work with the inevitable suffering.

We are working to Understand, embody and execute the seven qualities of the 21st Century Operating System for Success[14]: Empathy, vulnerability, humility, inclusiveness, generosity, patience, and balance in their Leadership style.

The downside of this work has to do with the kind of attention people pay to their lives after going through a transformational experience. There's a kind of 'filet of soul' that happens when we return back to our lives and work, and the people we know don't understand or honor what we've been through. Sometimes it seems like the only option is to either jump ship or go back to a being flat and mechanical. When we evolve, sometimes our old work lives don't fit anymore. It's great for the individual, but not for the organization that paid for the professional development experience. I always recommended that pairs or groups of professionals attend together, so that they would have a support system for integration when they returned back to work.

That was until the golden era of MatrixWorks in the workplace, when I started being invited into corporations to train groups. We found that the work environment can become a naturally therapeutic environment that allows us to bring forth our best, and our best can create the organization and a world that is human-friendly. Teams would fall so in love with each other that their best came forward. In three months teams would become so creative and change so much and then go back to the larger organization and it was unbearable for them because they had the direct experience of what health was possible. And that's where so many people would have to leave. While I was working with the girls toy division at Mattel, my contact in that division got the idea to expand our leadership training throughout the organization, and created an innovation program called Platypus. After the Platypus program was featured in the Wall Street Journal[15], everyone was so excited and energized. Mattel's leader called my contact to talk about Platypus, and said: "it's going great, everyone's happy, but the truth is I don't know how to lead this way. It can't go anywhere." The open source, non-hierarchical, open system wasn't going to fit for him. She said "thank you for letting me know," and she left to broker the program to Proctor & Gamble as Clay Street. The conclusion is that the big mammoth companies aren't going to be able to change without commitment to something larger than profit, and they lose great talent as a result. The orientation is embedded in the code of the system, communicating in a way that harmonizes or creates discord for the parts of the system.

Practice: Dream Company[16] Exercise

A dream company is one where:

You can be yourself.
You're told what's really going on.
Your strengths are magnified.
The company stands for something meaningful.
Your daily work is rewarding.
Stupid rules don't exist.

These 6 Virtues of a dream company come from research on 300 executives conducted by Rob Goffee and Gareth Jones. A company with these virtues would operate at its fullest potential through high levels of employee engagement. While these virtues may seem obvious, few companies actually possess all of them and many companies have counter-intuitive practices.

MatrixWorks has had the opportunity to use this model in several businesses with remarkable success. Their universal appeal makes the practice accessible to people working at any level of an organization. The process below outlines how to use the virtues as a diagnostic tool for your workplace.

A simple test to evaluate your workplace:

- Write each of these 6 Virtues on a sheet of paper.
- Use a scale underneath each one, numbering 1-5, with 1 being the least and 5 representing the most.
- Reflect on the scores you have assigned to each one.
- For any score of 3 or less, be curious why you think this is so.
- What is one action that could raise these lower scores to at least a 4, if not a 5?
- For any scores marked at 1, what meaning do you make of this? How will you intervene to help your business/workplace move in the direction of a 'dream workplace'?

Groups Gone Bad
Shadows in Group Life

Not all groups are good. We're not just being 'Pollyanna' here in thinking everything is going to be wonderful. Less developed groups more often serve as a powerful force of pain. And some of the most painful experiences that human beings can have come from groups that have become toxic. In the history of MatrixWorks, both in business and organizations and in community groups, the primary factor of a group becoming toxic resides in the failure of the group and the leader to balance *autonomy and interconnectedness*. An imbalance of autonomy happens when too many differences show up without a unifying purpose, when each individual holds their own agenda in higher importance than that of the group. An imbalance of interconnectedness occurs when everyone is on the same page, at the expense of their own uniqueness and diversity. This power can also default to the leader. A typical phrase for this phenomenon is that the group has fallen into "group think." The devastation group think can cause is exhibited by the Challenger disaster of 1986. The space shuttle exploded during launch after leadership insisted on sending it, even after gaining warning from one engineer about a part that he suspected would cause the shuttle to explode unless launched in different weather conditions. In situations like this, where listening is overlooked in a system, the life of the system is silenced.

A healthy group system[17] will serve life, while a monoculture system (think: GMO's) where diversity is lacking will inevitably become dysfunctional. Problems arise when group members no longer feel that they can disagree with the views being espoused by the leadership. And that applies whether the view is good or bad, but people can't challenge it. Members will lose their curiosity and not balance inquiry and advocacy, because why advocate our point of view when feedback isn't valued? If leadership is over identified with a part, and they mistake the part for the whole, then they will create difficulties in collaboration.

3 important levels of toxicity within a group:

- Cults: Lack of healthy balance between autonomy and interconnectedness. Powerful and charismatic leaders or teachers who act as the most important part of the group end up infantilizing members. People seen as Gods are disempowering for the whole system to respond and bring the gifts of the parts. In the 21st century, leadership is too complex for one person and need the gifts of every person.
- Hijacking: Not skillfully working with chaos or failure to work with chaos. Having knee-jerk reaction of withdrawing or shutting down when the energy becomes intense.
- Betrayal: When the scapegoat archetype is loose in the group so that there's a continuous process of looking for the person whose fault it is, rather than seeing the dysfunction in the system. With the scapegoat archetype, if someone is scapegoated in a group or as a group, there is an experience of betrayal that relationship and connection is not safe. If you cast someone out of the system, the system will find the next scapegoat, and the next person elected to carry the scapegoat will be the person least integrated into the matrix.

The inability to harvest the evolutionary impulse of chaos in a group will have one of two possibilities: either the group will become flat, unexpressive, and no one will care anymore, or the group will escalate, explode, and disband. It will either sweep the problem under the rug, act like nothing is happening, ignoring the elephant in the room, or there will be a traumatic hot button where nothing gets accomplished.

Members may still be present but the group won't be able to sequence into the next evolution of itself. Flatness will keep amplifying, but there won't be resolution or higher evolution that integrates both parts of the polarity. Until group participants can have the experience of being safe in a group, so that they have a different experiential reference point, it will continue to happen because it's in their field.

It is important to acknowledge the truth that some groups go bad. When a group doesn't fulfill it's potential, we can either attempt conscious healing as a whole, or leave. We can shift away from the blame game into more curiosity and inquiry. If we can identify the pattern that keeps repeating itself, we can work with it. Continuous chaos and conflict are always signs of a system that's broken. If you find yourself in one of these groups and you're not successful in bringing the group out of its toxicity, think about ending your membership and getting yourself into a group that's safe. It's always okay to leave and find a group that resets your system, because the right group will find space for you again.

Practice: If you're trying to help a group move out of its toxic state, you might experiment with introducing the emergence cycle, and see if the group can understand what is the natural rhythm of a healthy group.

Reflection Question: Do a scan of your most challenging and most inspirational groups. For those that were more challenging, notice which of the principles we've identified were present or operating? Looking back, can you imagine an intervention that could have helped this group become a living system? What would have needed to happen?

Emergence

In the group, I experienced a kind of consciousness that was almost a singularity, like a dropping of personalities and a joining together where there was no sense of conflict. Nobody was in opposition and everybody was just helping each other. It became obvious that we weren't responding to individual personalities but were responding to something much deeper, much more real in each other that was collective, something that we shared-a commonality, really. There was a tremendous sense of listening and awareness that was much greater and much more vast than anything I've ever experienced. And with that experience came a sense that there was just one body in the room.
- Jane Metcalfe

E mergence is a meta-skill throughout the work: in every moment, in every intervention and every group. Emergence invites us into new potential.

Emergence happens when we have enough safety for feedback, enough diversity for complexity, and enough vision, intention, and purpose for evolution.

The emergent cycle is a map[18] of how change occurs in living systems:

- Large-scale change begins with local, isolated activities.
- These local activities become viable, they inspire other actions.

- Local actions networked together learn from each other and grow in effectiveness.
- Suddenly, always unpredictable, the network leaps to a new level of capacity and influence.
- This emergent force is far stronger then anything imagined or predicted by local efforts.
- This new force wields tremendous influence, changing things everywhere, both locally and globally.
- Tinkering cannot change emergent forces. New countervailing forces must be created to replace them.

Emergence is the indication that a group is alive, and participating in harmony with all life. Emergence is the competency to read the invisible intention, needs, and possibilities of the group and invent new structures that support creative flow. MatrixWorks facilitation mastery means borrowing the structures and exercises that are helpful, and inventing new ways of working with the group. It is the coupling of relational responsiveness to the group and creative freedom of expression.

Outcomes

In closing, we leave you with a hope to create healthy relationships and groups, and the capacity for self-regulation in any context. Going forth, we offer a template for defining what success means to you. We recommend taking your time to reflect and listen deeply for what comes from your true self. Then, reflect on what maps you've learned that will help you get there.

MY SUCCESS PLAN

NAME:

PURPOSE: What is your higher purpose?

MISSION: What is your mission? This builds upon your purpose, and should be more specific and tangible. It should also be something others will easily understand.

TRANSFORMATION: What is the specific transformation you are working to catalyze and support in your clients or customers?

VISION: What is your Vision? What would be a 12 on scale of 1 to 10?

WHY: Why is this vision important to you? How would this vision make your life better? What will it give you?

FEELINGS: One of the primary ways to stay motivated and focused on achieving your vision is to remind yourself how you will feel when the vision has become a reality. So how will it feel? Come up with at least three juicy descriptions of how you will feel.

GOALS: How will you know when your vision has been achieved? How will you measure your success? What measurable goals would you like to set? It's good to have at least one long term (1 year or longer) goal and at least one short term (4 months or less) goal. They should be realistic and achievable, yet enough of a stretch to be exciting. Make a short but powerful list of goals; and set a target date for each one.

CELEBRATION: What will you do to celebrate and reward yourself for achieving each goal? Planning this ahead of time can make the process more fun.

OBSTACLES: What obstacles or challenges are you facing now? What challenges might you face in the future on the way to your vision? Make a list. Include both outer and inner challenges. Outer challenges include things like lack of cash flow and inner challenges include things like bad habits or limiting beliefs.

BEING: Who do you need to be in order to overcome those obstacles and achieve your vision? What "qualities of being" will help you be successful? Who will you need to become in order to catalyze and support the transformation you are committed to in your clients?

STRATEGIES AND PROJECTS: What general strategies would lead to achievement of your vision and goals? Also, what specific strategies could you use to overcome each obstacle from above? Make a "menu" of possibilities. At this stage you don't need to evaluate or commit to these strategies. Just brainstorm a list.

ACTIONS: Actions are the specific tangible steps you will take to implement your strategies. Make a massive action plan. It is good to have a large menu of possible actions to choose from.

Again, at this stage you are not evaluating or committing to specific actions. Make a list of actions that will absolutely produce results. Include actions that you will do once and actions that you will do repetitively.

CHOOSE AND COMMIT: Now go back through your Strategies and Actions brainstorms and underline each strategy and action that you are committed to implementing. Ask yourself which 20% of these actions will get 80% of the results. Choose the ones that have the most likelihood of producing results efficiently and do them first.

STRUCTURES: Goals are much easier to achieve when you have support structures in place. Some examples are: post a motivating display where you can see it often, enroll in a training course, enroll a support buddy, join or start a mastermind group, schedule a regular time each day or each week to work on your goals, structure your time and organize your physical space so that it is most supportive, set up tracking systems to monitor your follow through and progress, hire part time people to help with very specific things, and get the right software tools in place.

TEAM: What roles do you need filled in order to effectively implement your strategies and projects? Who are the best people to fill those roles?

SOFTWARE: What software functions need to be fulfilled? What are the best software options to meet your specific needs?

NEXT STEPS: What actions will you take in order to use this new clarity and inspiration to get the ball rolling immediately and build some momentum. What will you do today? This week?

NOURISHMENT: How will you remember to pause and allow nourishment and satisfaction to be a part of the success process?

Summary

The Ground: Theory

Basic goodness: People are basically good, treat them (and yourself) that way, including at work. Not all systems support basic goodness, but we always have access to transformation. We can reach the natural great perfection by resting in our basic goodness and mimicking living systems.

Living systems: Diversity of unique parts, interconnected relationships, and emergent self-creation characterize living systems. Just like the natural world, people are living systems and work better in environments that support life. Industrial environments like the assembly line support machines, which we are not.

5 friends: People need safety, support, truth, creativity, and value in work life and relationships. Without these friends, we won't get very far in our groups.

Neuroscience: Knowing what is going on inside of you helps to understand social triggers and how to work with them. Neuroscience validates the necessity of love and safe connection in work.

4 pillars: Paying attention to the body, subtle energy, relationships, and the field, will result in groups working in a living and sustainable way.

Essential Patterns: All generative relationships constantly go through a cycle of connection, chaos, and creative evolution.

The Path: Facilitation

Facilitation Mastery: Group facilitators are not creating connection and belonging, they are merely making it visible and more sustainable.

Self-Regulation: anything living is constantly modulating itself. Knowing your own shadows, triggers, and monsters under the bed will help you work with others.

Geometry & Weaving the Matrix: Organizing the group so that every person has the opportunity to deeply connect with every other member will give the direct experience of how living systems work. Whole system interconnectedness will create the feeling that the whole is greater than the sum of its parts.

Tracking: A facilitator is always paying attention to the group energy, and then making contact with members about their experience so that the energy can flow through the system and express health.

Planning and Design: Designing a plan with context, container, and content in mind will help you adapt our theory to your unique groups and leadership style. Powerful practices to include in your design are:

- [ ] Connection, Chaos, Creative Evolution
- [ ] Group projects that use every member as a different body system
- [ ] Perturbance, Intention and Impact, Feedback
- [ ] Polarities, Archetypes, Scapegoating, and Victimhood
- [ ] Enactments for individuals and small sub-groups
- [ ] Success plans using a particular model they've learned to apply in their particular work and life situation

The Fruit: Practical Application

Going Forth: Great suffering exists in all pockets of the globe. In order to respond to this need for healing, our societies need stronger communities and networks, our communities need stronger tribes and teams, our teams rely on strong individuals, individuals must connect with themselves. Enlightened Feminine energy is critical in Leadership during this time in history. If we are to thrive as a species, we must learn to work together with more care, compassion and creativity by putting Love back into Leadership.

Wounding in Groups: Not all groups are healthy. Some are traumatic, but don't project past experiences onto new possibilities. It's possible to create new forms of group organization that are life-affirming and serve life!

Emergence: Make a plan for success going forward. Find allies to support your work. Emergence is always happening when you apply the recipe of living systems: creation, differences, and relationships.

MatrixWorks: All living systems are constantly evolving in relationship to their environment. Creativity and invention are essential parts of this work. When all parts of a group system are included and celebrated for all of who they are, when life is nurtured, and when we listen to the whispers of what wants to emerge, then we are working in a MatrixWorks way.

Additional "Evocative One-Liners" for Facilitators

The following is a list of advanced tools for MatrixWorks Facilitators. These may not all be relevant to you or your groups. Pay attention to the lines that jump out at you and spark your interest.

1. In the beginning, safety/trust and each person's WANTING are primary.
2. Take care to support the design of the universe through the group: from core to periphery and periphery to core.
3. If someone "doesn't know," physicalize it to invite insight.
4. When a group seems to run by itself, a theme has emerged/ appeared and is being worked by the group.

5. Tracking is always directed toward what/who is present and what/who is absent.

6. To the person doing the process, it is always about "me."

7. Co-facilitators function well when not captured by their own self-doubt.

8. Co-facilitators also function well by emotionally resonating with the group and group members and by being aware of their own impulses.

9. Co-facilitators can remember that experience changes the brain.

10. Pay attention to who goes "last" and help this not become a pattern.

11. When a group member is "most out," allow them to enter thru a channel of the matrix, rather than be made to feel something is wrong, i.e. that they are a "mess."

12. Be willing to tolerate a period of "low energy" as the group unconscious builds potency to move to a new level.

13. Be creative regarding getting information into the Field underneath the "radar" of the defenses.

14. Letting go of doubt allows us to recognize timeless awareness.

15. Trying hard, efforting, is not helpful.

16. Without doubt, tension, efforting, the truth of non-separateness is easier to feel.

17. Red, Yellow, Green light metaphor is empowering to group members.

18. We are authorized to take our own "name tags" with us into any group, put them on and assume a role that will make us more awake, responsive and capable.

19. Name polarities in the group and use the potency of relational magnetism: Aloneness vs. Loneliness; Non-Separateness vs. Co-Dependency.

20. Name what is happening in a creative way: "There's a Hot Spot"; "Internal Squeeze"; "Flying Fishes"; The 'M Theory': mother, matrix, magic; etc.

21. In a Hot Spot, be willing to be Radical. Watch out not to be captured by bewilderment and freezing.

22. If a group member or whole group is in the Fight/Flight response, re-engage the Social Nervous System via offering connection in very simple ways: eye contact, simple touch, sensations, very simple words. Stay away from complexity and too much cognitive focus. Use the language of a 6 yr. old. Go for the simple kernel of truth: "you felt hurt"

23. When the Social Nervous System is re-engaged, name this by saying something like: "we are out of the danger zone," "we are back in connection"

24. After a conflict is worked, help the group savor the relaxation/relief that is in the living present of its return to connection.

25. Help the group know it is developing stamina to tolerate the natural tension that exists between who we are and who we are becoming: between our present health/wholeness and our woundedness and between the health and vulnerability of who we are becoming.

26. You want to be "hired" by the Adaptive and Wise Group Unconscious. This requires your willingness to be a "fool," and becoming sensitive to the slightest urging/whisper from this adaptive and wise Unconscious (also called the Deep Mind).

27. Remember everything (almost) is workable!!!

28. Check to see if you act like you believe in a Living World?

29. Are you willing to let go of everything so something new can come?

30. If you are overcome with devotion, will you bow?

Closing
Integration and Conclusion

*There is almost a sensual longing for communion with
others who have a larger vision. The immense fulfillment
of friendship between those engaged in the evolution of
consciousness has a quality almost impossible to describe.*
-Pierre Teilhard de Chardin

We want to create an environment where the fruit merges with
the ground, where the whole cycle recreates itself. The fruit is
inherent in the ground.

The real fruit is the direct experience of the truth of
interconnectedness, and the embodiment of the dynamic balance
between connection and autonomy. The fruit ripens where there is no
doubt that I have a place at any table. When I know how to gently and
respectfully nudge people to move over so I have the place that I want.
When I am more myself than I was when I joined this group. The fruit
is what Tibetan teacher Chogyam Trungpa Rinpoche called being a
full human being in connection and relationship. When the fruit is ripe
and everyone has a place at the table, we can actually accomplish more.

Working with living systems, we are working with the questions
of life, and the fruit is the answer to those questions. These are fluid
and moving answers, like a call and response. There's a need, a desire,
and a way to fulfill it. We ask each other: What do you want? What
do you need? We already know that the answer will be: I want to be

all of who I am. I want to belong. I want to offer my gifts to the world. Hakomi means, "who are you?" The fruit is the resolution that there are no more questions.

Our work points to a totally different state of consciousness beyond discursive knowledge. You can know without knowing how you know. The more you begin to work in this way, the more synchronicity, magic, and flow happens. This teaches us how to live well. And you come to know you're not in charge and there's no way you could have orchestrated it.

To really integrate a new worldview there needs to be a structure of support for this new possibility. As groups, facilitators, and organizations, we are called to create a structure going forward by making use of the small group in evolutionary circles. We all need a support group to maintain any habit, in order to socialize the habit. For any intervention to take root, it has to take form in your life. We encourage you to interpret these teachings creatively for your own life and leadership context. May we all live to see the healthy emergence of ***groups rising*** in our lifetime.

MatrixWorks is an open, living system that welcomes the creativity of its practitioners in fostering health for their unique group context. MatrixWorks is a nurturing environment thst grows the potential of individuals and groups. Any time you are fully yourself, accepting the other, in balanced relationship, in the present moment, and orienting towards health and healing, you are working in a MatrixWorks way.

In closing, we hope this MatrixWorks manual is useful for your study and practice of the power of small groups. Learning to work with Groups as Living-Systems supports the true value of being human, and is key to cultivating cultures of connection and compassion.

For more information, visit www.matrixworks.org

Reading list

Supplemental Resources for Continuing Exploration

Aposhyan, S.; Natural Intelligence; Body-Mind Integration and Human Development, 1999

Barkin, K.; Corporate DNA, 1998

Benson, J.; Working More Creatively with Groups, 2009

Brown, Juanita The World Café: Shaping our Futures Through Conversations that Matter, 2005

Capra, F.; The Web of Life, 1997

Merton, T.; Belonging to the Universe, 1993

Clippinger, J.; The Biology of Business, 1999

Conley, Chip: PEAK: How Companies Get Their Mojo from Maslow, 2007

Colman, Arthur: Up from Scapegoating: Awakening Consciousness in Groups, 1995

Cooperrider, D.; Appreciative Inquiry: A Positive Revolution in Change, 2005

Flaherty, J.; Coaching: Evoking Excellence in Others, 3rd edition, 2010

Goleman, D.; Working with Emotional Intelligence, 2000

Social Intelligence, The New Science of Human Relationships, 2007

Johnson, Steven; Emergence: the Connected Lives of Ants, Brains, Cities, and Software, 2002

Johnson, Sue: Hold Me Tight; Emotionally Focused Couples Therapy, 2008

Kahane, A: Power and Love: A Theory and Practice of Social Change, 2009

Kayser, T.; Mining Group Gold, Third Edition: How to Cash in on the Collaborative Brain Power of a Team for Innovation and Results, 2010

Kelley, S.; The Complexity Advantage, 1999

Koestenbaum, P.; Leadership: The Inner Side of Greatness, 2002

Lemkow, A.; The Wholeness Principle: Dynamics of Unity Within Science, Religion, and Society, 1990

Levoy, G.; Callings; Finding and Following an Authentic Life, 1998

Lewis, Th. MD; A General Theory of Love, 2001

Lipman-Blumen, J.; Connective Leadership: Managing in a Changing World, 2000

Hot Groups, 1999

Macy, J.; Coming Back to Life: Practices to Reconnect Our Lives, Our World, 1998

Masaru, E.; Messages from Water and the Universe, 2010

McClure, B.; Putting a New Spin on Groups: The Science of Chaos, 2nd edition, 2004

Mindell, A.; Sitting in the Fire: Large Group Transformation Using Confict and Diversity, 1995

Mindell, A.; The Leader as Martial Artist: Techniques and Strategies for Revealing Conflict and Creating Community, 2000

Ornish, D.; Love and Survival: 8 Pathways to Intimacy and Health, 1999

Oshry, B.; The Possibilities of Organization, 1986

Seeing Systems: Unlocking the Mysteries of Organizational Life, 2007

Pascale, R.; Surfing the Edge of Chaos: The Laws of Nature and the New Laws of Business, 2001

Porges, S.; Polyvagal Theory, 2011

Sawyer, Keith.: Group Genius: The Creative Power of Collaboration,

Senge, P.; The Fifth Discipline Fieldbook: Strategies and Tools for Building a Learning Organization, 1994

Senge, P.; The Dance of Change: The Challenge of Sustaining Momentum in Learning Organizations, 1999

Siegal, D.; The Developing Mind: How Relationships and the Brain Interact to Shape Who We Are, 2001

The Mindful Brain: Reflection and Attunement in the Cultivation of Well-being, 2007

Sills, F.; Craniosacral Biodynamics: The Breath of Life, Biodynamics, and Fundamental Skills, 2001

Simmons, A.; A Safe Place for Dangerous Truths: Using Dialogue to Overcome Fear and Distrust at Work, 2006

Smith, Kenwyn K. and Berg, David: Paradoxes of Group Life: Understanding Conflict, Paralysis, and Movement in Group Dynamics. 1997

Swimme, B.; The Universe Story: From the Primordial Flaring Forth to the Ecozoic Era--A Celebration of the Unfolding of the Cosmos. 1994

Tharthang Tulku; Kum Nye Relaxation, Vol. 1, Vol. 2

Thich Nhat Hanh; Transformation and Healing: Sutra on the Four Foundations of Mindfulness, 2006

Tulku Thondrup; Boundless Healing, 2001

The Healing Power of Mind, 1998

Waugh, B.; The Soul in the Computer: The Story of a Corporate Revolutionary, 2001

Weisinger, H.; Emotional Intelligence at Work: The Untapped Edge for Success, 2000

Wheatley, M.; Leadership and the New Sciences: Discovering Order in a Chaotic World, 3rd edition, 2006

A Simpler Way, 1998

Turning to One Another: Simple Conversations to Restore Hope to the Future, 2009

Whyte, D.; Crossing the Unknown Sea: Work as a Pilgrimage of Identity, 2002

Zohar, D.; ReWiring the Corporate Brain: Using the New Science to Rethink How We Structure and Lead Organizations, 1997

Endnotes

1   Matrix means "womb" or "mother", and correlates to a safe and nourishing environment in which people in groups can experience healing and a deep sense of belonging.

2   Hakomi is a therapeutic practice that means "how do you stand in relationship to all that is?" It uses the body as a living system, which we will explore further in the following chapters.

3   Being able to direct attention and to choose our focus opens up new possibilities. Only looking at what's in front gives one slice of reality, expanding attention to include what's happening beyond this room to perceive something larger. Then I can practice true leadership: leading self where a better creation can emerge.

4   Dr. Dan Siegel, http://www.drdansiegel.com/resources/wheel_of_awareness/

5   In Buddhism, these are considered to be the causes of suffering.

6   Again, why humility is so important!

7   Adapted from Hakomi Training Materials from Ron Kurtz and Rob Fisher.

8   An emotional trigger; an impairment to regulation of psychological processes.

9   The capacity to pay attention to the present moment without any judgment

10   Other examples include: "Relationship is all there is," "You can be fully yourself and a full member of this group"

11   For me, committing to a daily spiritual practice (however wonderful or lousy I may feel or show up) helps create a pathway of opening to something larger than myself.

12   Volatile Uncertain Complex Ambiguous: This term was coined by the military to describe the conditions we are now working in.

13   ADAPTED FROM U THEORY--OTTO SHARMER.

14   From The Athena Doctrine

15   http://www.wsj.com/articles/SB10233051812889347920

16   From "Creating The Best Workplace On Earth," Rob Goffee and Gareth Jones, Harvard Business Review, May 2013

17 As we explored earlier with living systems, a living system in health will balance creation, diversity, and relationships. The Challenger decision showed an imbalanced bias towards creation, without focusing on diversity of opinion or relationship.

18 Adapted from the work of Margaret Wheatley - Authentic Leadership Class